A Kentucky Gathering

Recipes
&
Remembrances

by

Judith Ralph / Kim Mitchell

Remembering Home...
Judith Ralph

"... indeed my heritage is
beautiful to me." Psalm 16:6
Kim Mitchell

International Standard Book Number 0-9718928-0-6
Library of Congress Card Catalog Number 2002109140

Cover design and book layout by James Asher Graphics

Manufactured in the United States of America

Hen House Press in association with

All book order correspondence should be addressed to:

Hen House Press
4341 Hawesville Rd.
Reynolds Station, KY 42368
E-mail inquiries: jhenhousepress@AOL.com
To Order Call: 270-233-4237 or 270-233-4274

Contributors

Jerl Dean Miller Adkins
Reynolds Station, KY
Aunt of co-author/illustrator

Julie Ralph Alford
Reynolds Station, KY
Daughter of co-author/illustrator

Denzil Back
Morehead, KY
Uncle of co-author

Foy and Judy Back
Winchester, KY
Parents of co-author

Redgie Back
Cabot, AR
Uncle of co-author

Stephen Back
Lexington, KY
Brother of co-author

Kathryn Baily
Big Woods, KY
Cousin of co-author

Phyllis Blanton
Wellington, KY
Aunt of co-author

Linda Brothers
Bardstown, KY
Sister-in-law of co-author

Katie Browning
Fern Creek, KY
Niece of co-author

Kathy Jo Motley Cole
Ezel, KY
Cousin of co-author

Barbara Coomes
Whitesville, KY

Martha Sue Ralph Edge
Fordsville, KY
Cousin-in-law of co-author/illustrator

Sharon and Lori Harris
Hartford, KY

Vicki Hawes
Narrows, KY

Pamela Ralph Howard
Former resident of Hartford, KY
Now residing in Nachitoches, LA
Sister-in-law of co-author/illustrator

Shelia Isaac
Big Woods, KY
Cousin of co-author

Anna Mary Leach
Owensboro, KY
Great-aunt of co-author/illustrator

James Lexter and Joyce Leach
Owensboro, KY
Great-uncle and aunt of co-author/illustrator

Minnie Bell Basham Leach
Fordsville, KY
Late great-grandmother of co-author/illustrator

Norman and Thelma Wright Matthews
Fordsville, KY
Cousins of co-author/illustrator

Lydia Susan Midkiff
Fordsville, KY

Clarence Carlisle Miller
Fordsville, KY
Grandfather of co-author/illustrator

Kathryn Mitchell
Fern Creek, KY
Mother-in-law of co-author

Ralph Mitchell
Reynolds Station, KY
Husband of co-author

Richard "Mutt" Mitchell
Fern Creek, KY
Late father-in-law of co-author

Charles and Emogene Miller Moseley
Whitesville, KY
Parents of co-author/illustrator

George "Red" Moseley
Owensboro, KY
Uncle of co-author/illustrator

Stanley and Dorothy Moseley
Owensboro, KY
Great-uncle and aunt of co-author/illustrator

Evelyn Motley
Ezel, KY
Cousin of co-author

Martha Motley
Frenchburg, KY
Cousin of co-author

Mary Kathryn Motley
Ezel, KY
Cousin of co-author

Hubert Oliver
Owensboro, KY

Andrew Ralph
Whitesville, KY
Father-in-law of co-author/illustrator

Dennis Ralph
Reynolds Station, KY
Husband of co-author/illustrator

Martha Carmon Ralph
Fordsville, KY
Sister-in-law of co-author/illustrator

Ruby Ralph
Former resident of Hartford, KY
Now residing in Nacitoches, LA
Mother-in-law of co-author/illustrator

Debra Hobbs Richards
Fordsville, KY
Cousin of co-author/illustrator

Tom Schultz
Louisville, KY
Dear friend of co-author

Willa M. Spradling
Big Woods, KY
Cousin of co-author

Shelia Oliver Thurman
Utica, KY
Cousin of co-author/illustrator

Lorene Leach Wright
Fordsville, KY
Great-aunt of co-author/illustrator

Mandy Perkins Wright
Hartford, KY

Brenda Oliver Young
Lexington, KY
Cousin of co-author/illustrator

Dedications

*T*his cookbook is dedicated to my mother, Emogene Miller Moseley, whose generous hospitality, home-cooking and love for family inspired its contents, and to my father, Charles Moseley, whose philosophy of hard work and unrelenting determination has enabled me to move forward.

And to my husband Dennis, the father of our three beautiful children, and the faithful husband whose sacrificial love has freed me to follow my dreams. Thanks! ! !

Judith Moseley Ralph

I want to thank my parents Foy and Judy Motley Back, for establishing in me early in life, the essential priorities. To my dad, whose steadfastness in the Word and love for God, has shown me that success comes in putting Him first. To my mom, who has always put her family before self and before others, showing me that the love of my family is more important than the approval of others.

And finally to my husband Ralph, who has beautifully established these very standards within our boys and me. You are our rock.

Kimberly Back Mitchell

January

A season of remembrance

*"…and a book of remembrance was written
before him for them that feared the Lord, and
that thought upon his name." Malachi 3:16*

Willie Edgar and Minnie Bell Basham Leach

Year 2001-Day 1-Month 1

"I'm 78 - plus years - three fourths of a century. One thing I say about being older is one has more memories than the younger generation. I'm amazed at the number that's not old enough to remember when the stock market crashed in 1929, the Big Depression hit in the 1930s, the WPA work program was initiated by Uncle Sam, when the Japanese bombed Pearl Harbor on December 7, 1941, or when F. Roosevelt was elected to the 3rd and 4th terms. I remember when as a young lad I would be anxious for the first day of May - we, my sisters and I, could take off our shoes (we got one pair a year) and go barefoot for the summer - ground felt so cool to the bottom of my feet. We had no car, no radio, no newspaper, no lawyers - a person's word was their bond - nothing had to be in writing. We had plenty of time to visit our neighbors, to go church, to sit by the fireplace at night and talk."

James Lexter Leach

"Pap would go to town (Fordsville) on Saturday afternoon with a bunch of men and play 'sell pitch' in the old tobacco warehouse. It was kindly against the rules to play cards. Back then repivals were held in tents, mostly by the Baptists, and the preachers were always preaching against playin' cards, dancin', and a'drinkin' that moonshine."

James Lexter Leach

Sally's Quick and Easy Lasagna

(This recipe is borrowed from a true Italian cook)

1½ pounds ground round
4 cups spaghetti sauce
1½ cups water
15 ounces ricotta cheese
16 ounces mozzarella cheese
½ cup Parmesan cheese, grated
2 eggs, lightly beaten
¼ cup fresh chopped parsley
¼ teaspoon black pepper
8 ounces lasagna noodles, cooked and drained

Preheat oven to 400 degrees. Brown and drain meat. Add spaghetti sauce and water. Bring to boil, reduce heat, cover with lid and simmer for 10 minutes. While sauce is simmering, mix together ricotta cheese, mozzarella cheese, Parmesan cheese, eggs, parsley and pepper. Generously oil a 13x9 pan. Put 1 cup sauce into pan. Top with 3 noodles, then 1½ cups sauce. Spread ½ of cheese mixture over sauce. Repeat steps ending with sauce. Cover tightly with aluminum foil. Bake 60 minutes. Remove foil, bake an additional 10 minutes.

Debra Richards

Fried Wild Rabbit

Dress a cotton-tail or swamp rabbit. Wash thoroughly, cut up and cover with salt water. Cook until near done. Remove, salt, roll in flour, then fry in a skillet of lard.

Judith Ralph

"*Many afternoons when I came home from school, my terrier would meet me. He would chase rabbits until they were exhausted and run into a burrow or up into a tree hole. I took a green briar, ran it up into the hole to catch hold of the rabbit's fur and pulled him out. If that didn't work, I built a fire and smoked him out. We would have rabbit for supper the next night.*"

James Lexter Leach

Skillet Cabbage

1 head cabbage, chopped
4 tablespoons lard
½ teaspoon sugar
Salt and red or black pepper to taste

Fill a large skillet with about an inch of water. Bring to a boil. Add cabbage, lard, sugar and seasonings. Cover and simmer for about 25 minutes.

Judith Ralph

Hoppin' John

2 cups dried black-eyed peas
½ pound salt pork, cut into small pieces
2 cups chopped onion
1 cup chopped green pepper
2½ cups water
1 cup uncooked long-grain rice
Salt and pepper to taste

Sort and wash peas; place in a large pot. Cover with water 2 inches above peas; let soak for 8 hours or overnight. Drain. Return peas to pot; add salt pork, onion, and green pepper. Cover with water, and simmer, covered, 2 hours or until peas are tender and water has cooked very low. Add 2½ cups water, rice, and seasonings to peas. Cover and cook over low heat 20 minutes or until rice is done.

Kimberly Mitchell

Nutty Broccoli Slaw

1 package chicken ramen noodles
16-ounce package broccoli slaw mix
2 cups sliced green onions
1½ cups chopped fresh broccoli
6-ounce can ripe olives, drained and sliced
1 cup sunflower seeds
½ cup slivered almonds, toasted
½ cup sugar
½ cup cider vinegar
½ cup olive or vegetable oil

Set aside the noodle seasoning packet. Crush the noodles and place in a large bowl. Add slaw mix, onions, broccoli, olives, sunflower seeds, and almonds. Toss. In a jar with a tight-fitting lid, combine contents of seasoning packet, sugar, vinegar, and oil. Shake well. Drizzle over salad and toss.

Kathy Jo Motley Cole

"My great-uncle, Lexter Leach, contracted typhoid fever after visiting a neighbor boy whose sister had fallen ill with the fever. He had been warned before entering the house.

All winter he lay in the bed; his frail body fighting for life. The town doctor instructed Mam to allow her son to sip one half cup of buttermilk three times daily and at midnight if he was awake. Soon his sister Lorene became victim to the fever. Both should have died, but the Lord willing they both survived and continue to live now into their 80s. Looking back, Lexter believes ones course in life is determined by the choices one makes."

Judith Ralph

Thoughts from Uncle Redge

A cure for asthma – find a willow tree. Cut a limb off the same height as the child. Hide the stick. When you outgrow the stick, you outgrow the asthma.

A cure for poison ivy - juice of a milkweed plant.

A cure for headache - rub snakeroot between your fingers, then smell.

An insect repellent – rub snakeroot between hands, put on face.

Stomach problems – boil Queen of the Meadow and make into a tea. Drink.

Sty for eye – yellow root. Also, lay a flax seed in the corner of your eye.

Stomach worms – 1 teaspoon turpentine and sugar. Mix together and drink.

Car sickness – a couple of tablespoons of sauerkraut juice will settle your stomach.

Mutt's Cornbread

We chose to publish this recipe in its original wording in order to preserve its character.

2 cups meal
1 cup of flour
1 large tablespoon salt
3 teaspoons baking powder
1 egg, if you like
1 tip of soda on end of teaspoon, if milk is sour
2 tablespoons sugar

Use 1 tip of sinnumon on teaspoon, if you wish; Be sure to soda according to milk; how sour it is. Mix ingridence. Sift 3 or 4 times. Beat well

The late Richard "Mutt" Mitchell

Skillet Corn Bread

1 tablespoon oil
Iron skillet
1½ cups self-rising cornmeal
½ cup self-rising flour
1 egg
1 cup buttermilk

Preheat oven to 400 degrees. Put skillet with 1 tablespoon oil in oven while mixing cornbread batter. Mix all ingredients, pour into hot skillet. Bake 20 to 25 minutes or until golden brown.

Judy Back

Snowball Cake

2 envelopes unflavored gelatin
4 tablespoons water
1 cup boiling water
1 cup granulated sugar
20-ounce can crushed pineapple, drained
Juice of 1 lemon
3 packages Dream Whip
1 large angel food cake

Dissolve gelatin in 4 tablespoons water. Add 1 cup boiling water. Add sugar, pineapple and lemon juice to gelatin mixture. Mix well. Chill until partially jelled. Whip 2 packages Dream Whip according to package directions. Add Dream Whip to gelatin and mix well. Trim the brown edges from the cake and cut cake into small cubes. Line a large bowl with plastic wrap. Alternate cake cubes and mixture, one after the other. Chill overnight; turn out on plate and frost with 1 package prepared Dream Whip. Keep refrigerated.

Phyllis Blanton

"Don't tell a dream until after you've had breakfast, for fear it might come true."
Ralph Mitchell

Mamaw Back's Dropped Doughnuts

3 cups all-purpose flour
1 tablespoon baking powder
1 teaspoon salt
½ teaspoon cinnamon
¼ teaspoon nutmeg
2 tablespoons vegetable shortening
1 cup sugar
2 eggs
1 cup milk
4 cups oil
Confectioner's sugar

Sift first 5 ingredients into a bowl and set aside. In medium bowl cream shortening and sugar. Beat in eggs, 1 at a time. Alternate milk and flour mixture, stirring until well blended. Heat oil; carefully drop batter, ¼ cup at a time into oil. Turn doughnuts as they brown evenly. Remove and drain on paper towel-covered racks. When cool, toss with sugar in a paper bag. Makes 13 to 15 doughnuts.

Kathryn Bailey

Hot Cider Punch

Hot cider is as much a tradition on New Year's Eve in our family as cabbage and black-eyed peas are on New Year's Day.

1 gallon apple cider
6-ounce can orange juice concentrate
1 package red hots candies

Mix and heat until red hots are melted.

Judith Ralph

Sentimental Snickerdoodle Cookies

1 cup soft shortening
1½ cups granulated sugar
2 eggs
2¾ cups sifted all-purpose flour
2 teaspoons cream of tartar
1 teaspoon baking soda
½ teaspoon salt
2 teaspoons cinnamon
2 tablespoons sugar

Blend shortening, sugar, and eggs together. Sift together dry ingredients and add to the creamed mixture. Roll dough into balls the size of a walnut. Roll balls in a mixture of 2 teaspoons cinnamon and 2 tablespoons sugar. Place balls 2 inches apart on ungreased cookie sheet. Bake at 400 degrees for 8 to 10 minutes. Makes about 6 dozen cookies.

Phyllis Blanton

Aunt Phyllis used to babysit my brothers and me when we were little. Their farm allowed for many a summer adventure. With 4 children of her own plus the 3 of us, she was always baking something to keep up with our appetites. Snickerdoodle Cookies were just one of the many great things she would make. Years later when I found myself in Eastern North Carolina and homesick, I would make Snickerdoodle Cookies. Needless to say, they never tasted quite like Aunt Phyllis'.

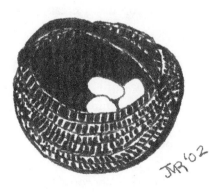

Martha Motley's Marshmallow Roll

This recipe was in my grandmothers collection. After she died, I have cherished her recipes. Just by reading all her "sweet treats" brings back wonderful childhood memories of her kitchen and the comforting smells.

½ pound graham crackers, finely crushed
1 cup chopped dates
1 cup chopped nuts
1 cup finely-chopped marshmallows
½ pint whipping cream

Mix graham cracker crumbs, reserving ⅓ for coating, dates, nuts, and chopped marshmallows together. Pour in cream and mix well. Form into a ball. Coat with saved crumbs. Roll tightly in wax paper. Chill in the icebox for 24 hours. Slice and serve.

Kathy Jo Motley Cole

Foy Back

Brother Foy's Cream Candy

3 cups granulated sugar
1 cup heavy cream
½ cup water

Mix well the sugar, cream, and water in a large cooker. Set temperature on high heat until it comes to a full boil. Reduce to medium heat until the temperature of candy reaches 260 degrees. Remove candy from the heat and pour on a cold, well-buttered marble slab. When candy is cool enough to handle, begin to pull. At this point add a prayer. Continue to pull until candy begins to become hard to pull. Stretch it into a long piece and then lay it on a piece of wax paper and cut into small pieces with scissors.

Foy Back

Snow White Snow Cream

2 tablespoons vanilla
3 tablespoons sugar
1 egg, well beaten
1 large bowl of fresh snow

Mix together the vanilla, sugar and egg. Add to the bowl of snow.

Judith Ralph

"*In 1917, we moved on the Henry Hobbs Farm, that was up the road toward Newton Springs. We lived in the upper house two years. That was when the First World War was. I had an uncle in it, Jess Keown. We had a stove; had to cut wood for it. My dad took a load of tobacco off and it come a two foot snow and ice on top of that thick enough to hold a horse up. He couldn't get back home for a while. Me and my brother and mother had to keep the stove burning and we had a cow to milk and feed and water. We had plenty of food in the house.*"

"*In 1921, we moved up there by Newton Spring Church on my uncle's farm, Floyd Keown. We still went to Highland School. It was about 3 or 4 miles. We walked every day. If it came a big rain we'd pull our shoes off and wade the creek. Sometimes it had ice in it.*"

Clarence Miller

February

A season of hearts

*"That their hearts might be comforted,
being knit together in love…"*
Colossians 2:2

Clarence and Velma Miller, Leamon and Myrtle Craig, Lorene and Paul Wright,
Anna Mary Leach, James Lexter Leach

"I Wouldn't Mind the Chiggers"

On quiet nights, by candlelight,
My thoughts begin to flow;
Across the fields I dearly love,
Now blanketed with snow.

I remember when the grass was green,
I covered every mile.
When I look back upon those times,
It always makes me smile.

My feet were bare, my toes were skinned,
And all the world looked bigger.
If I could recall those peaceful days,
I wouldn't mind the chiggers.

Kathryn Bailey

Swiss Steak

Round steak, tenderized
Salt
Pepper
Flour
Vegetable oil
Onion
Tomato sauce or ketchup

Buy tenderized round steak and cut into pieces. Salt and pepper and flour heavily. Add oil to skillet and brown steak on both sides. Place browned meat in a roaster. Add 1 slice of onion to each piece of meat. Add flour to the skillet where you browned the meat, making a gravy. Pour the gravy over meat. Add tomato ketchup or tomato sauce to the meat. Add a little water. Bake at 350 degrees until tender.

Joyce Leach

"When we lived on the Miller farm, the girls were of courting age. When their fellows came to call on them, they would sit in the front room, or parlor as we called it, all day long. They did not even come out to eat. Mama did get where she would bake a cake and serve them a slice, though. I found this interesting and would peek in the window to see what they were doing. When it was time for the boys to leave, Papa would drop his shoe on the floor. It was a disgrace for the boys to stay past 9 p.m."

James Lexter Leach

Kentucky Hot Brown

2 tablespoons butter, melted
¼ cup flour
2 cups milk
1 cup grated sharp cheddar cheese
¼ teaspoon salt
½ teaspoon Worcestershire sauce
1 pound sliced, cooked turkey
8 slices toast
8 slices bacon, cooked
8 slices tomato
4 ounces Parmesan cheese

Melt butter in saucepan. Add flour; stir well. Add milk, cheddar cheese, and seasonings. Cook, stirring constantly until thick. Arrange turkey on toast and cover with cheese sauce. Place sandwich under broiler until sauce begins to bubble. Garnish with crumbled bacon and tomato slices. Sprinkle with Parmesan cheese. Serve immediately.

Kim Mitchell

If you bump hoes together, you'll be workin' together next year.

Potato Soup

My mom would make this for my papaw. She would purée the celery and onions because he wouldn't eat them if he could see them. This was his favorite.

½ cup chopped onion
½ cup chopped celery
4 to 5 potatoes, peeled and cubed
2 cups chicken broth
1 stick butter
1½ cups flour
2 cups milk
10¾-ounce can cream of chicken soup

Boil onions and celery in broth until they are really tender. Remove from broth and purée after they have cooled slightly. Cook the potatoes in the chicken broth until soft. Remove from heat. In another saucepan melt butter and stir in flour. Add milk into this rue and heat until thick. Pour this mixture into potatoes, onion, and celery. Add soup. Heat thoroughly. Salt and pepper to taste.

Mandy Perkins Wright

"Sometimes when we woke up in the morning in the old house, snow covered our beds and a bucket of water sitting on the hearth would be frozen over. We had to thaw it out before making the morning coffee. The fireplace was big, as tall as a man could reach, but it was not efficient. A man could sit right next to it, burn up on one side and freeze to death on the other. I remember popping popcorn in that big old fireplace by holding a bucket of shelled kernels over the fire with a tobacco stick."

Charles Curtis Moseley

Homemade Soda Crackers

4 cups bread flour, sifted
½ teaspoon soda
1 teaspoon salt
1 cup butter
¾ cup sour milk

Sift dry ingredients together. Cut butter into sifted ingredients. Gradually add just enough sour milk to make a stiff dough. Knead thoroughly 8 to10 minutes. Roll out onto lightly-floured board to about 1/5-inch thick. Cut in rounds or squares. Punch holes in top of cut-out dough, using the tines of a fork. Place on greased baking sheet. Bake in preheated 400 degree oven 12 to 15 minutes. Makes about 3 dozen crackers.

Willa M. Spradling

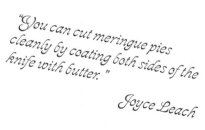

"You can cut meringue pies cleanly by coating both sides of the knife with butter."

Joyce Leach

Sweet and Sour Water Chestnuts

(An appetizer that my great-aunt likes to make)

Three 5-ounce cans water chestnuts
1 pound bacon
3 tablespoons cornstarch
4 tablespoons water
2 cups sugar
1 cup water
1 cup vinegar
½ teaspoon salt
½ teaspoon pepper

Cut large chestnuts in half: use small ones as is. Cut bacon in 3 sections. Wrap chestnuts in bacon, securing toothpicks. Bake 45 minutes at 350 degrees, or until bacon is crispy. Mix cornstarch and water. Boil sugar, 1 cup water, vinegar, salt and pepper for 5 minutes, then add cornstarch. Cook until thick and clear. Pour over chestnuts and bacon and serve warm.

Mandy Perkins Wright

Sugar Molasses Syrup

1½ cups sugar
¾ cup water

Combine ingredients and boil until it thickens, approximately 3 minutes. This is delicious over hot buttered biscuits or pancakes.

Judith Ralph

"*In February, we went down to where the sugar trees grew and tapped them for sap. We drilled holes in the trees and plugged them with a piece of cane or with a corncob. If we used a corncob, we first burned off the fuzz, then bored a hole through the center. The sap drained into buckets. Mom boiled it down to make maple syrup or cooked it down to make little sugar cakes for a sweetener. Sugar cakes looked a little like brown sugar. One barrel of sap made 1 gallon of syrup.*"

Norman Matthews

Cold Bread Pudding

4 cups bread cubes
2 cups milk
2 eggs, beaten
⅛ teaspoon salt
½ cup light brown sugar
1 teaspoon vanilla
¼ teaspoon nutmeg
½ cup raisins

Sometimes when we came home from school, especially on cold wintry days, Mama would have a pan of cold bread pudding waiting for us.

Combine bread and milk in a large mixing bowl. Stir in eggs, salt, sugar, vanilla, and nutmeg. Mix well. Add raisins. Pour into buttered baking pan. Bake in a 350-degree oven for 25 minutes.

Emogene Miller Moseley

To Emogene,
I love you little
I love you lot
I love you like
A little pig loves slop.

From Mother

Sourdough Starters

Old Time Starter

2 cups unsifted plain flour
2 tablespoons sugar
1 tablespoon salt
1½ cups water
1 tablespoon vinegar

Combine all ingredients in a crock. Mix well; set in warm place until thoroughly sour, about 12 hours.

Modern Starter

½ package dry yeast
2 tablespoons sugar
2 cups all-purpose flour
2½ cups water

Combine all ingredients in a crock, let stand in warm place, covered, approximately 2 days. Refrigerate starter when not in use. Replenish with 2 cups warm water and 2 cups flour.

Flaky Homemade Biscuits

2 cups all-purpose flour
2½ teaspoons baking powder
½ teaspoon salt
⅓ cup shortening or lard
¾ cup milk

Sift together flour, baking powder and salt. Cut in shortening with fork until it resembles course cornmeal. Add the milk and blend lightly with a fork until flour is moistened and dough pulls away from the sides of the bowl. Turn out on a lightly-floured board. Knead lightly and roll ¾-inch thick. Cut dough with biscuit cutter, dipping cutter into flour between cuts. Place on a lightly-greased pan and brush tops of biscuits with a little bacon grease. Bake at 475 degrees for 12 to 15 minutes. Makes twelve 2-inch biscuits.

One of my sweetest memories of Mamaw Back was watching her make homemade biscuits, which she did every morning. She would pull this large crock lined with flour, out from under the cabinet. She added more flour, a few more ingredients, a little milk from the cow she had milked earlier that morning, and stirred. In just a few minutes a cookie sheet was completely filled with little cutouts of dough all the same size. Just before popping them into the oven she would take a spoon, dip it into the bacon grease, and spread it over top of the biscuits. The crock would go back under the cabinet, to my amazement, never needing to be washed out. Just as I delighted in these biscuits years ago, my youngest son, Anthony, now enjoys them ever as much.

Kimberly Mitchell

Carrot Cake

(Well worth the extra trouble)

4 cups grated carrots
2 cups sugar
1 cup butter
½ cup water
2½ cups all-purpose flour
1 tablespoon cinnamon
2 teaspoons baking soda
2 teaspoons ground cloves
¾ teaspoon ground allspice
¾ teaspoon nutmeg
½ teaspoon double-acting baking powder
½ teaspoon salt
2 eggs
½ cup raisins (optional)
½ cup pineapple, crushed and drained (optional)
1 cup pecans or walnuts, chopped

Preheat oven to 350 degrees. In a 2-quart saucepan, combine first 4 ingredients and bring to a boil, stirring. Reduce heat to low and simmer for 5 minutes, stirring. Let cool. Into a large bowl sift all dry ingredients. In another large bowl beat 2 eggs until they are lemon-colored; add carrot mixture and the flour mix with nuts and fruits. Stir until just combined. Divide batter between 2 buttered and wax-paper lined loaf pans and bake in a preheated 350 degree oven for 35 to 40 minutes or until a cake tester comes out clean. Cool in pans for 5 minutes. Remove to wire racks and complete cooling. Dust with sifted sugar and serve. (Or you may choose to add the delicious frosting on the next page)

Cream Cheese Icing

8 ounces cream cheese, room temperature
¾ cup powdered sugar
2 tablespoons butter, room temperature
2 tablespoons milk
½ teaspoon vanilla extract

Mix all ingredients thoroughly; add more milk, one teaspoon at a time, if necessary. Spread on cooled carrot cake and sprinkle with chopped nuts.

Kim Mitchell

Tunnel of Fudge Cake

1½ cups butter, room temperature
6 eggs
1½ cups granulated sugar
1½ cups flour
1 package Pillsbury's 2-layer-size double Dutch fudge butter cream frosting mix
2 cups chopped walnuts

Nuts and frosting mix are essential to the success of this cake. Cake has a soft fudge candy-like interior and brownie-like texture.

Cream butter in large mixing bowl at high speed. Add eggs, one at a time, beating well after each. Gradually add sugar; continue creaming at high speed until light and fluffy. By hand, stir in flour, frosting mix, and walnuts until well blended. Pour batter into greased tube pan. Bake at 350 degrees for 60 to 65 minutes. Cool completely, 2 hours, before removing from pan and serve.

Phyllis Blanton

Quickie Cherry Pie

This recipe was given to me in the late 1950s. It is easy to make on a busy day and has been one of Charles' favorite.

1 stick margarine
1 cup self-rising flour
1 cup sugar
1 cup milk
Two 16-ounce cans red tart pitted cherries in water
¾ cup sugar
½ teaspoon cinnamon
1 teaspoon vanilla extract

Melt margarine in a 2½-quart baking dish and set aside. In a medium bowl mix flour, sugar and milk until smooth. Pour this mixture into the buttered baking dish. Sweeten the cherries with the sugar and add cinnamon and vanilla extract. Stir and then pour this cherry mixture over the flour mixture in the baking dish. Bake in 375-degree oven 45 minutes or until brown. Crust will rise to top of pie.

This is also great made with peaches. Instead of cherries, use two 15-ounce cans of peaches in syrup, stirring in the cinnamon and vanilla extract.

Emogene Moseley

"The first time I ever ate canned, or for that matter, any kind of pineapple was at Aunt Myrtle's house when she lived in Owensboro. She always wanted us to have new experiences and to 'educate' us about life outside the country."

Emogene Miller Moseley

Raisin Pie

My papaw loved this!

1½ cups raisins
½ teaspoon lemon juice
1 cup milk
2 egg yolks, reserve the whites for meringue
2 tablespoons flour
1 cup granulated sugar
1 baked pie shell

Cover raisins with just enough water to cover, add lemon juice and boil for 5 minutes. Drain. Add milk, egg yolks, flour and sugar. Heat until thick. Pour into cooled pie shell. Top the pie with meringue. Bake at 400 degrees until lightly brown.

Mandy Perkins Wright

"When Daddy was young, chivaree was a common thing. When a wedding took place, friends would kidnap the bride and groom after the ceremony to keep them apart. Daddy said a neighbor man was put in a hog box on his wedding night and loaded into a wagon. The men backed the wagon up to a lake, pretending to dump the groom. The groom made such a racket, the horses were spooked and he was dumped into the water. He nearly drowned before his friends could get him out."

Dennis Ralph

March

A season of rebirth

"That ye put off concerning the former…and be renewed in the spirit of your mind."

Ephesians 4:22,23

Roger Wells, Lenore and Grimsey Rose, Foy Back

Grandma Wright's Meatloaf

1½ pounds ground beef
1 pound pork sausage
1 teaspoon salt
Pepper to taste
1 small onion, finely chopped
1 cup oats
1 cup soda crackers, crushed
½ cup tomato catsup
1½ cups milk, or enough to moisten the ingredients
2 teaspoons sugar
2 large eggs

Sauce

½ cup tomato catsup
½ cup brown sugar
¼ cup chopped green peppers
¼ cup chopped onion

Mix first 11 ingredients together. Form into one large, or two regular size loaves. Mix sauce ingredients together. Pour over meatloaf. Bake at 350 degrees for 1 hour or until desired doneness.

You may use a sugar substitute in place of brown sugar.

Thelma Wright Matthews

"*When I was a baby, Grandma Wright made me a pacifier by wrapping a piece of fat in a cloth.*"

"*Rhoda Alice Menges Wright, my grandmother, was a small woman, about 4'11" tall. I remember watching as she carefully cut paper sacks into neat little squares, rolled tobacco up in them, then licked the edges to seal the tobacco inside. She would twist the end to keep the tobacco from falling out then light it up and smoke the handmade cigarette. She began smoking after the doctors told her that paper sacks contained iodine and iodine would help her goiter.*"

Thelma Marie Wright Matthews

Chicken Croquettes

¼ cup butter or margarine
¼ cup plus ⅓ cup all-purpose flour, divided
1 cup milk plus 1 tablespoon milk, divided
½ teaspoon salt
⅛ teaspoon pepper
2 cups minced, cooked chicken
1 egg, beaten
1 cup soft bread crumbs
Vegetable oil

Melt butter in a heavy saucepan over low heat. Add ¼ cup flour, stirring until smooth. Cook 1 minute, stirring constantly. Gradually add 1 cup milk, cook over medium heat, stirring constantly, until thickened and bubbly. Stir in salt and pepper. Remove from heat; stir in chicken. Cover and chill about 1 hour. Shape chicken mixture in 6 balls or logs. Combine egg and 1 tablespoon milk, mix well and set aside. Dredge croquettes in ⅓ cup flour; then dip into egg and milk mixture and coat each croquette with bread crumbs. Fry croquettes in deep hot oil (370 degrees) for 3 to 5 minutes or until golden brown. Drain croquettes on paper towel. Yield: 6 servings

Kim Mitchell

Broccoli Cornbread

10-ounce package frozen broccoli, thawed and drained
1 small onion, finely chopped
1 stick margarine, melted
8-ounce carton cottage cheese
3 eggs, beaten
1 box Jiffy cornbread mix
1 tablespoon finely chopped jalapeño pepper
¾ teaspoon salt

Mix all ingredients well and pour into a greased 8x12 glass baking dish. Bake in preheated oven at 350 degrees for 45 minutes.

Emogene Miller Moseley

Deb's Potato Salad

5 pounds potatoes
4 eggs, boiled and peeled
¾ cup salad dressing
1½ tablespoons mustard
¼ cup pickle relish
1 teaspoon dill pickle juice
½ teaspoon dill seed
¼ teaspoon mustard seed

Peel, dice and boil potatoes until done (test by piercing potato with a fork). Drain, peel, and dice boiled eggs and mix with remaining ingredients, including the potatoes. May be served warm or cold.

Debra Hobbs Richards

"Going to my Grandmother and Old Daddy Oliver's farm was always a special event in my life. Knowing that Banana Salad was a favorite of mine, Grandmother made it every time I visited. In my mind's eye, I can still see the sparkling, cut crystal bowl full of rich, yellow Banana Salad waiting to be savored by our entire family, especially me!"

Banana Salad

1 stick butter
¾ cup sugar
2 tablespoons vinegar
2 eggs, beaten
Dash of salt
4 bananas
½ cup chopped peanuts or pecans

In a saucepan over very low heat, melt butter. Add sugar, vinegar, eggs and salt. Stir continually over low heat until sauce thickens. Remove from heat, let cool. When sauce is cool, pour over cut up bananas. Add ½ cup chopped peanuts or pecans.

Sheila Oliver Thurman

Baked Fruit

29-ounce can peach halves
29-ounce can pear halves
20-ounce can pineapple tidbits
6-ounce jar maraschino cherries
1 stick butter
½ cup brown sugar
2 teaspoons curry powder
½ cup coconut or sliced banana

Arrange fruit in a 9x13 inch baking dish. In saucepan melt butter and brown sugar. Stir. Add curry powder and coconut or banana. Stir. Pour over fruit. Bake at 325 degrees for 1 hour.

Dorothy Moseley

Lucy's Green Cheesecake

"I got this recipe in the 1960s from my neighbor and friend, Lucy Evans, the first time we went to her home for a card party. She served this cheesecake and it has been a favorite of mine for parties, holidays and week-ends ever since."

12-ounce can evaporated milk
3-ounce package lime gelatin
1 cup boiling water
32 graham crackers
6 tablespoons margarine
1 cup plus ¼ cup sugar, divided
8-ounce package cream cheese, room temperature
1 teaspoon vanilla extract
Juice of 1 lemon

Chill 1 large mixing bowl, beaters from electric mixer, and evaporated milk in freezer while mixing other ingredients.

Mix lime gelatin with boiling water and set aside to cool. Crush graham crackers for the crust. Melt the margarine. Combine graham cracker crumbs, melted margarine and ¼ cup sugar. Press the mixture into a 9x13x2-inch baking dish.

Cream together cream cheese, 1 cup sugar, vanilla and juice of 1 lemon. Whip evaporated milk and then blend in other ingredients. Pour mixture into crust and chill.

Emogene Miller Moseley

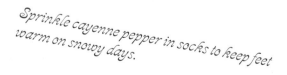

Sprinkle cayenne pepper in socks to keep feet warm on snowy days.

Oatmeal Cake

1¼ cups boiling water
1 cup quick cook oatmeal
1 stick margarine
1 cup granulated sugar
1 cup packed brown sugar
2 eggs
1 teaspoon cinnamon
1 teaspoon vanilla
1 cup flour
1 teaspoon baking soda

Topping

3 tablespoons melted butter
1 cup brown sugar
3 to 4 tablespoons cream
2 egg yolks
1 cup coconut
1 cup finely-chopped pecans

Pour boiling water over oatmeal. Let stand 20 minutes. Cream margarine and sugars in large mixing bowl. Add eggs, cinnamon, and vanilla. Mix well. Stir in oatmeal mixture. Add flour and baking soda, mixing well. Bake in 9x13-inch pan at 350 degrees for 30 to 35 minutes.

For topping cream melted butter, brown sugar, cream and egg yolks. Add coconut and pecans. Stir well. Spread over hot cake and bake an additional 10 minutes or until coconut is brown.

Kathryn Mitchell

"*Mom tells the story of how she first came across an Oatmeal Cake recipe. Dad and she married in 1962. She was 16 and he was 19. Dad was working at J.C. Penney for $1.00/hr. Needless to say, times were hard. One day while at work, Dad spotted a piece of paper on the floor; it was a recipe for Oatmeal Cake. For the next several weeks, each time Mom would go to the grocery store, she would buy one ingredient from the recipe, bring it home, then put it away. Finally, when all the items for the cake were purchased, she baked the Oatmeal Cake.*"

Kim Mitchell

Chess Pie

½ cup butter or margarine
1½ cups sugar
3 eggs
1 teaspoon vinegar
1 teaspoon cornmeal
1 teaspoon vanilla
9-inch unbaked pie shell

Cream butter and sugar together, beat eggs in one at a time. Stir in vinegar, cornmeal, and vanilla. Pour into pie shell and bake 30 minutes at 350 degrees. This is delicious.

Kathryn Mitchell

Bess Murphy always knew who was recovering from illnesses in our small community of Ezel, KY. A tin of these chewy brownies was always the best medicine.

Bess Murphy's Blonde Brownies

1 cup sifted all-purpose flour
½ teaspoon baking powder
⅛ teaspoon salt
½ cup butter or shortening
1 cup packed brown sugar
1 slightly-beaten egg
1 teaspoon vanilla
½ cup chopped nuts
½ package semi-sweet chocolate chips

Sift flour, baking powder and salt together. Set aside. Melt shortening in saucepan. Remove from heat and mix in sugar. Add 1 tablespoon water if vegetable shortening is used. Stir in egg and vanilla. Add nuts to flour mixture. Mix to coat nuts. Gradually stir flour mixture into the sugar mixture. Mix well. Sprinkle chocolate chips over batter. Gently fold into batter. Spread into greased 9x9 pan. Bake at 350 degrees for 20 to 25 minutes.

Kathy Jo Motley Cole

Liniment

1 part vinegar
1 part alcohol
1 part turpentine

Let alcohol eat up 1 cake camphor gum before adding to other ingredients.

This recipe for liniment was taken from the notes of Myrtle M. Mayer, then Huffman, around 1946.

Peanut Butter Cookies

½ cup shortening
½ cup peanut butter
½ cup granulated sugar
½ cup brown sugar
1 egg, well beaten
1½ cups self-rising flour

I often baked these cookies for school and church parties when the kids were small. They are still a favorite of my son Andrew.

Mix first 5 ingredients together, thoroughly. Blend flour into mixed ingredients. Chill dough. Roll into 1-inch balls. Place approximately 3 inches apart on a baking sheet. Flatten with a floured fork. Bake for approximately 10 minutes at 300 degrees. Note: Do not overcook; bake until set but not browned. Makes 2 to 3 dozen.

Judith Ralph

Sassafras Tea

4 red sassafras roots, each about 2 inches long
1½ quarts water

Scrub the roots well, rinse thoroughly and remove bark. Place roots, root scrapings, and water in a large saucepan. Bring to a boil, reduce heat, and simmer for 15 minutes. Turn off heat and let steep for 10 minutes. Strain, then serve.

Judith Ralph

"There are two types of sassafras, red and white. The root from red sassafras is boiled into a tea for drinking. Its bark produces a stronger tea for colds. Tea made from white sassafras is not good to drink. It is said that white sassafras is 'only good for bean poles.'"

Hubert Oliver

"When I was young, my grandmother, Charlie A. Oliver, would boil up a tea made from sassafras roots, and would serve it to me hot. It was pink in color. It was supposed to be a blood tonic and also good for bronchitis."

Brenda Oliver Young

"When we moved to the Miller farm, there were saplings as big around as your fist, growing on the hill beside the house. Pap cleared the 8-acre field for raising corn. It was during the Depression and we could not afford to buy fertilizer for the crop. That only produced nubbins for our brown Guernsey milk cow that received 6 nubbins and a handful of corn fodder daily. Pap never raised hay. She in turn, produced a meager 4- pound lard bucket of milk 2 times a day for our family. I often think about that old milk cow and how she was born into depression just like us kids."

James Lexter Leach

April

A season of beginnings

*"Though thy beginning was small,
yet thy latter end should greatly increase."*

Job 8:7

Dennis and Judith Ralph, Julie and Jimmy Alford
Charles Andrew Ralph, and Robert Ralph

"Old Red"

When I was a kid down on the farm,
Chore time I sure did dread.
We had a fighting rooster, and
That rooster's name was Red.

He had spurs two inches long,
And sure thought he was tough.
I was scared of that old rooster,
He made my mornings rough.

I would sneak out around the barn,
As quiet as a mouse.
But sure enough, here would come,
Old Red and chase me to the house.

Old Red chased my mom one day,
She hit him with a stick of wood.
Old Red *was* a tough old rooster,
But the dumplin's sure were good.

Kathryn Bailey

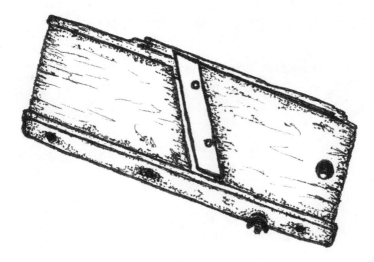

JVR '02

Swedish Meatballs

3 to 5 pounds ground chuck
2 cups quick oats
2 eggs
½ teaspoon pepper
1 teaspoon chili powder
1 teaspoon garlic salt
½ cup chopped onion

Sauce

2 cups ketchup
2 cups brown sugar
1 teaspoon garlic salt
½ cup chopped onion
1 teaspoon liquid smoke

A friend and co-worker, Linda Chapman, prepared these tasty meatballs for my daughter's wedding reception in April 1999. They were a real winner with a blend of tomato flavor and a hint of spice.

Mix first set of ingredients together. Roll into ½ to 1-inch balls. Place in a baking pan. Combine ingredients for sauce in a medium saucepan. Cook over medium heat. Boil for 3 minutes. Pour sauce over uncooked meatballs. Bake at 350 degrees uncovered for 40 to 45 minutes. Note: may freeze ahead of time, thaw and heat. Makes 160 to 300 meatballs.

Judith Ralph

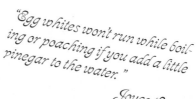

"Egg whites won't run while boiling or poaching if you add a little vinegar to the water."

Joyce Leach

"When we moved to the farm you couldn't see a house no place. There were elms, hickories, and cedars everywhere. When we started the new house in '46, we went into the woods and cut logs from virgin timber to be sawed for lumber. We dragged them out of the woods with mules and pulled them up the hill by trolley. Sometimes we had a log rolling. That's when folks got together and sawed lumber for a house or to burn as fire logs. In those days, neighbors helped each other."

Simply Salmon Salad

14¾-ounce can salmon
2 to 3 tablespoons prepared mustard
¼ cup vinegar
1 teaspoon sugar
16 soda crackers, crushed
1 boiled egg, sliced

Mix first 5 ingredients, then top with egg slices. Chill.

The late John Moseley
Submitted by George "Red" Moseley

John James and Ester Moseley

Barbecued Spareribs

4 to 5 pounds small, meaty spareribs
2 large sliced onions

Barbecue Sauce

½ cup ketchup
1½ teaspoons salt
¼ teaspoon hot sauce
⅛ teaspoon chili powder
1 cup water
½ teaspoon dry mustard
1 tablespoon brown sugar

Place a layer of small, meaty spareribs in bottom of heavy kettle. Cover with a layer of sliced onions. Mix sauce ingredients. Pour barbecue sauce over top. Repeat layers. Cover and bake at 325 degrees until middle is tender. (2 to 2½ hours) Uncover the last ½ hour. Serve hot.

Kathryn Mitchell

"A few drops of lemon juice added to simmering rice will keep the grains separate."
Joyce Leach

Wilted Lettuce

Leaf lettuce
¼ cup sliced green onions
3 radishes
6 slices bacon
2 tablespoons vinegar
2 tablespoons water
½ teaspoon salt
⅛ teaspoon pepper
1 teaspoon sugar
2 tablespoons bacon drippings

Tear lettuce into salad bowl. Add green onions and radishes.
Fry bacon until crisp. Drain and crumble. Add vinegar,
water, salt, pepper, and sugar to drippings and bring to boil.
Pour over lettuce and green onions. Add crumbled bacon
and toss lightly. Serve while hot.

Judith Ralph

"On Friday nights, Mama would fry up a bunch of fish that we had caught. Sometimes there would be as many as 20 to 30 people gathered around the kitchen table, men first, followed by the women and children. Back then a person could catch a lot of fish. Fish don't bite like that these days."

Dennis Ralph

The first year we were married, Dennis cleared a little spot in our backyard for a "truck patch." He planted radishes, onions, and leaf lettuce in a 6' by 6' plot, which he prepared by burning off grass, leaves and weeds to kill unwanted seed.

Country Fresh Ketchup

3 heads cabbage
3 red peppers
3 green peppers
4 onions
6 green tomatoes
2 quarts vinegar
Sugar to taste

This recipe was given to me by Inez Rudd. She spent her life cooking and raising a family of 13 children. Her country ketchup is a wonderful addition for pinto beans or even hot dogs.

Chop vegetables fine; cook in sweetened vinegar. Cook until cabbage is about done. Put in jars and seal.

Kathy Jo Motley Cole

A Good Sauerkraut Relish

1 large can sauerkraut, drained and rinsed
1 cup chopped celery
1 large onion
1 cup sugar
½ cup vegetable oil
½ cup vinegar

Combine all ingredients, toss and chill.

Willa M. Spradling

Eggless, Milkless, Butterless Cake

1 cup brown sugar, firmly packed
1¼ cups water
⅓ cup shortening
1½ cups raisins
2 cups all-purpose flour
½ teaspoon soda
1 teaspoon baking powder
½ teaspoon salt
1 teaspoon cinnamon
1 teaspoon nutmeg
½ to 1 cup chopped nuts
1 teaspoon orange or lemon peel, grated

Preheat oven to 350 degrees. Combine first 4 ingredients, bring to a boil. Cook 3 minutes. Cool. Add sifted dry ingredients. Combine flour mixture to the liquid. Beat well, stir in nuts and orange or lemon peel. Pour into greased 9x13 pan. Bake 45 minutes. Cool.

Willa M. Spradling

"Wet tobacco leaves serve as a poultice for bee stings. I experienced this first hand one summer day when a bumble bee stung me on my mother's farm."

Brenda Oliver Young

Never-Fail Cupcakes

This is my earliest try at baking. The recipe came from a children's activities magazine.

1 egg
½ cup cocoa
½ cup shortening
1½ cups all-purpose flour
1 teaspoon vanilla
½ cup sour milk
1 teaspoon baking soda
1 cup sugar
½ cup hot water

Put in bowl in order given. Do not mix until last item has been added. Then beat well. Pour batter into lightly greased or lined muffin pans. Bake at 350 degrees for 20 minutes or until cake tests done. Makes approximately 24 cupcakes.

Mary Kathryn Motley

Reese Bars

2 cups creamy peanut butter
1 cup packed brown sugar
½ cup butter, melted
1 teaspoon vanilla
1 pound powdered sugar
1 cup chocolate chips
2 tablespoons butter

Mix peanut butter, brown sugar, melted butter, and vanilla together until smooth. Add powdered sugar a little at a time, until smooth and spreadable. Spread in a buttered 9x13 pan. Slowly melt chocolate chips and butter in microwave. Spread melted mixture over the peanut butter mixture. Let set. Cut into squares.

Willa M. Spradling

Preacher Pie

I made several of these pies to sell at our annual Sorghum Festival in Hawesville, KY. Both days I sold out.

1 egg, beaten
4 tablespoons sugar
1 tablespoon flour
½ teaspoon vanilla
4 tablespoons sorghum
1 tablespoon butter
Pecans or other nuts
Unbaked pie shell

Blend first 7 ingredients well. Pour into unbaked pie shell. Bake at 350 degrees for 35 minutes or until set.

Kimberly Mitchell

Aunt Lib's Caramel Pie

4 tablespoons butter
1 cup brown sugar
4 tablespoons flour
Pinch of salt
3 eggs, separated
1 cup milk
½ teaspoon vanilla
Pre-baked pie shell

Put butter in pan and melt. Mix sugar and flour together, add a pinch of salt. Add sugar and flour mixture to melted butter, mix well. Beat egg yolks. Pour milk and vanilla into beaten egg yolks. Stir well. Put in with sugar and butter. Mix well; cook until thick. Pour into shell.

Kathryn Mitchell

Chocolate Crispies

2 squares unsweetened chocolate, melted
½ cup butter
2 eggs, unbeaten
½ teaspoon vanilla
1 cup sugar
½ cup sifted flour
½ cup chopped nuts, optional

To melted chocolate, add butter, eggs, vanilla, sugar, and flour, beating well. Spread mixture in thin layer on a greased 12x16-inch baking sheet. Sprinkle with nuts, if desired. Bake at 350 degrees for 15 minutes. While still warm, cut into 2-inch squares. Cool and break. Great with a cold glass of milk.

Sheila Oliver Thurman

"While growing up on the farm, there was never any box brownie mix in our house. That was a luxury we could never afford. But Mama would make home-made Brownie Crispies. Now looking back, I realize that those brownies were far better than any box mix brownie ever could be. So here is Mama's Chocolate Crispies from the kitchen of Anna Mary Leach."

"A dampened paper towel or terry cloth brushed downward on a cob of corn, will remove corn silks."

Joyce Leach

A season of nurturing

"Her children arise up, and call her blessed..."
Proverbs 31:28

Debra Hobbs Richards, Flora Keown Miller, Judith Moseley Ralph

"Old Black Pocketbook"

Every place my mother went,
She took her old black pocketbook.
It held all the mysteries of life
But we weren't supposed to look.

She kept tissues for a runny nose,
An extra set of baby clothes,
You could find the deed to our old farm,
Also the title to the car,
A tube of lipstick, (seldom used),
Bobby pins and baby shoes, birth certificates
For the kids, (she had a lot of those).
Why she took the Castor Oil, heaven only knows.

I've often wondered and I think I'm right,
If I could only have taken a look,
The answers to the problems of the world,
Was in mom's old black pocketbook.

Kathryn Bailey

Since Dennis and I married in 1976, we have always gone to Mom's for Sunday dinner. She always fixes something special for every member of our family. We call it "Smorgasbord at Mom's." After the kids came along, she found that BBQ chicken was one of their favorite meats and could be easily prepared before church, so of course, this has become a regular dish on Sundays.

Sunday Dinner BBQ Chicken

1 whole chicken, cut into pieces
1 tablespoon vegetable oil
Salt and pepper to taste
18-ounce bottle of hickory smoke BBQ sauce

Arrange chicken pieces in lightly-oiled baking dish. Fill with approximately ½ inch of water. Season with salt and pepper. Cover and bake in 350 degree oven for about 1 hour. Remove from oven and add BBQ sauce. Cover and return to oven for 15 minutes. Then uncover and bake an additional 10 to 15 minutes until browned, but tender.

Judith Moseley Ralph

Crock Pot Barbecue

Roast, beef or pork
Salt and pepper to taste
1 onion, quartered
¼ cup water
18-ounce bottle barbecue sauce
1 tablespoon lemon juice
½ cup brown sugar

Salt and pepper roast. Place roast, onion, and water in crock pot. Cook overnight on low heat. Next morning, drain off broth. Chop roast into pieces and return to crock pot. Add barbecue sauce, lemon juice, and brown sugar. Cook all day on low heat. Serve on hamburger buns.

Kim Mitchell

Squash Casserole

3 cups sliced yellow squash, cooked
3 carrots, shredded
2 sticks margarine
1 large chopped onion
1 can cream of mushroom soup
Two 6-ounce boxes stuffing mix

Mix all ingredients together. Cook at 425 degrees for about 45 minutes in oven.

Judith Moseley Ralph

After Mamaw's death, Papaw remarried. At first, I thought I could never like this person who was supposed to replace my grandmother, but in time I realized that Katherine was not a replacement in our family - she was an addition. Katherine loved life, she loved to travel, and she loved family. She never failed to add laughter and good food to our gatherings. Among my favorites were her cream style corn and squash casserole made with fresh vegetables from Papaw's garden.

"My mother-in-law planted marigolds around the edge of her garden. It kept down insects on corn and beans."

Brenda Oliver Young

Pimento Cheese

2 pounds Velveeta cheese
1 large jar pimentos
5 or 6 large sweet pickles
6 eggs
¾ cup vinegar
½ cup sugar
1 tablespoon butter

Grate or grind first three ingredients together. Beat eggs thoroughly. Mix with vinegar and sugar over medium heat. Cook until thickened, stirring constantly. When thickened, add butter. Let cool and pour over cheese mixture. Chill.

Kathy Jo Motley Cole

Country Honey Mustard Dip

This is a great salad dressing.

½ cup mayonnaise or salad dressing
½ cup sour cream
2 tablespoons Dijon mustard
2 tablespoons honey

Mix all ingredients in bowl. Chill until serving time.

Kim Mitchell

Betty's Sweet 'N Spicy Dressing

1 cup mayonnaise
1 tablespoon olive oil
2 tablespoons wine vinegar
1 tablespoon horseradish mustard
1 tablespoon sugar

Stir all ingredients together, then chill. Pour over favorite lettuce salad. A zesty mixture of iceberg with romaine and endive lettuce compliments this sweet and spicy dressing.

Judith Moseley Ralph

This recipe is from the collection of Betty Sandefur of Olaton. She is a great country cook from the old school of whipping up fabulous dishes from little or nothing.

"At night when the frogs are croaking, you know they are a hollerin' for rain."

Andrew Ralph

"*My first childhood memory was of my Grandmother Miller. On hot summer days I remember seeing her walking from town to our house carrying melting ice cream cones.*"

"*The candy I remember her most often bringing was chocolate cordial cherries. There were three packaged like a candy bar.*"

"*When I stayed overnight with Grandmother Miller she always gave me money to take to the store and buy a can of Vienna sausages. When I was a child, these little wieners were not uniform in size and we always anticipated counting how many would be in a can.*"

"*At Christmas time, Grandmother Miller always had one big package for me. All year long she had bought and put items in the box. When looking through the box it seemed to be almost bottomless.*"

"*Grandmother Miller lived on a limited income. She had no indoor plumbing and heated and cooked with a coal stove. But she managed to save and purchase Series E. Savings Bonds for us grandkids. I used the bonds for a down payment on my first home after marriage, an 8' by 30' mobile home.*"

Jerl Dean Miller Adkins

"*We moved to Indiana so Daddy could work at the Chrysler Defense Plant during World War II. I remember we had ration stamps to get foods like sugar, coffee, and meats. My mother said you could not get a fresh chicken then; only a cold storage one and they weren't good. I also remember the family gathering around the radio and listening to the news about the war. My dad quit his job at the defense plant the day the war was over and we moved back home to Fordsville, KY.*"

Emogene Miller Moseley

Granny Cake

2 cups all-purpose flour
1½ cups granulated sugar
20-ounce can crushed pineapple, undrained
2 eggs
1 teaspoon soda
1 teaspoon salt
½ cup nuts
½ cup brown sugar

Icing

1 cup evaporated milk
½ stick margarine
½ cup sugar
1 teaspoon vanilla

Mix first 6 ingredients in bowl; pour into greased 9x13 pan. Mix together nuts and brown sugar; sprinkle over batter. Bake at 350 degrees 35 to 40 minutes. Let cool. While cooling mix together evaporated milk, margarine, sugar, and vanilla. Bring to a boil. Boil 1 minute. Pour over cake.

Willa M. Spradling

"Take a teaspoon of liniment mixed with sugar in a small glass of water for PMS."

Emogene Moseley

Strawberry Cake

1 box white cake mix
3-ounce package strawberry gelatin
¾ cup oil
½ cup water
4 eggs
½ cup strawberries, fresh or frozen

Mix all ingredients. Cook as directed on box.

Strawberry Icing

½ box powdered sugar
1 stick butter or margarine, softened
½ cup strawberries

Mix powdered sugar and butter until smooth and creamy. Stir in strawberries. Ice cooled cake.

Sharon Harris

"My grandmother Miller always gave me a piece of alum to hold on mouth ulcers which I frequently have. It looked like a clear rock and tasted terrible. Made you pucker-up!"

Jerl Dean Adkins

Sugar-Free Strawberry Pie

8 ounces cream cheese
1 teaspoon vanilla
5¼ teaspoons Splenda (sugar substitute), divided
1 graham cracker crust
1 cup cold water
2 tablespoons cornstarch
3-ounce box sugar-free strawberry gelatin
1 pint strawberries, hulled and sliced
Whipped topping, optional

Beat cream cheese, vanilla, 1¾ teaspoons Splenda until fluffy. Spread on bottom of crust. Mix water and cornstarch in small saucepan over medium heat until thick, about 1 minute. Add gelatin and 3½ teaspoons Splenda. Using a whisk, stir until gelatin is dissolved. Cool 10 minutes. Mix strawberries with gelatin mixture and pour over cream cheese layer. Whipped topping is optional.

Joyce Leach

Strawberry Pie

1 cup sugar
3-ounce box strawberry gelatin
3 tablespoons cornstarch
2 cups water
1 pint fresh strawberries, cleaned and sliced
1 baked pie crust

Mix dry ingredients and add water. Bring to a boil until it looks clear. Let cool and pour over fresh strawberries. Mix and pour into prepared pie crust. Chill.

Mandy Perkins Wright

My great-grandmother, Ruby Head loved to make desserts of all kinds. She always had a strawberry pie when she had fresh strawberries.

Mom's Chocolate Pie

2 egg yolks
1 cup sugar
3 heaping tablespoons flour
1½ cups milk
3 heaping teaspoons cocoa
1 teaspoon vanilla
1 baked pie shell

Cook first 6 ingredients until thick.   Pour into baked pie shell.

The late Mary Hillard

Mary Hillard
and friend

This recipe belonged to my mom, Mary Hillard. Mom was serious about her work, but she had a fun side, too. She could really dance the Charleston and each year on our birthday Mom put us under the bed. No one knows for sure how this tradition began.

Pie Crust

3 level tablespoons shortening
¾ cup self-rising flour
3 tablespoons ice water

Cut shortening into flour, add water and roll thin. Place into pie plate.

Joyce Leach

Chocolate Pie

1 cup sugar
3 tablespoons flour
Pinch of salt
3 tablespoons cocoa
2 egg yolks
1½ cups sweet milk
1 teaspoon vanilla
Butter or margarine, size of walnut
1 baked pie shell
2 egg whites
6 tablespoons sugar

Mix sugar, flour, salt, and cocoa together. Add egg yolks and milk. Mix well. Cook, stirring constantly until thick. Add vanilla and margarine. Pour into a baked pie shell. Beat egg whites until foamy. Add 6 teaspoons sugar. Beat until stiff. Pile onto pie and brown in hot oven.

The late Lydia Lavonia Webster Falk

"Fox grapes or wild grapes grow in the woods and are good for making jelly, wines, and marmalade."

Hubert Oliver

"*Sunday afternoons at my grandparents' house in Morton's Gap, Kentucky, were great times with relatives, good food and good conversations. That's how I grew up. My grandmother, Lydia Lavonia Falk, was a fantastic cook and made the best chocolate pie I have ever tasted! She never measured a thing, just put a bit of this and a dash of that, and the most beautiful meringue pie you ever laid eyes on was placed on the table. Her pies never lasted long. My grandfather, Talbert Clarence Falk, would always ask the blessing for the meal. Everyone filled their plates high with all the combinations of main dishes, vegetables, and salads that my mother, grandmother, and aunts cooked up.*"

"*Afterwards, we all drifted on out to the front porch. There were several chairs out there and a swing. The kids all made way to the swing and the older folks kicked back in the rockers and lounge chairs.*"

"*A train ran through the middle of town and my grandparents' house faced the train tracks. Every little bit, a train made its way through town blowing its whistle and the engineer would wave greetings to my grandparents. The thing I loved most about being there was listening to all the stories the older folks, my relatives, would tell. As we sat in the swing, gently swinging so as not to miss a word, my dad and Uncle Murphy would talk about their younger days when they used to work in the coal mines. One story I remember them telling was when my dad and his brother were just boys and they were playing ball. The ball hit my uncle in the head and knocked him completely out. Dad carried him in his arms all the way home. I remember this story vividly and it made me realize how much they loved each other as brothers. Some of the stories were spooky and gave us chill bumps. My Aunt Betty Lou was always laughing and her stories were funny. It was a good time to grow up – there with all my relatives- loving, caring, and sharing. Yes, Sunday afternoons at my grandparents' were great times!*"

Lydia Susan Midkiff

June

A season of pondering

*"Ponder the path of thy feet,
and let all thy ways be established."*
Proverbs 4:26

Emogene Miller Moseley and Charles Moseley

"*It has been told of 'Ole' Grandpa that he was an ornery old cuss, a young man who joined the Legions of Lee, and while imprisoned by the Yankees he would gladly have traded his daily ration of food for a fresh killed rat. He lived to the ripe old age of 100, which was quite an accomplishment for his day, and attributed his longevity to his daily toddy and to the fact that the 'Massa' must have had some plan for his life. However, Grandpa Moseley left a little more behind than his Civil War legacy and his good health for future generations. The older folks chuckle as they tell the tale of Grandpa Moseley and his encounter with the nosey neighbor women…*"

"*It was one of those summer days that was hot enough to fry an egg. Ole Grandpa was plowing tators with one of those mule-drawn plows when he looked up and noticed that the neighbor women were watching him from afar. He wiped the sweat from his brow and was about to return to his chore when one of the women yelled out, 'My, my, Mr. Moseley, you ought to be ashamed of yourself.' For, you see, he was wearing nothing but a long-tailed shirt.*"

"*He stood there for a moment, lifted his shirttail plumb over his head and calmly replied, 'Yes, ma'am I'm shore ashamed!'*"

Judith Ralph

"*Never wear a dress while plantin' tators, 'cause tators have eyes.*"

Dennis Ralph

"*Never put a cover on anything that is cooked in milk unless you want to spend hours cleaning up the stove when it boils over.*"

Joyce Leach

Tony's One Pot Sauce and Fixin's

Meat

20 pounds quartered chicken, whole pork roast or pork loin halved, and/or whole beef brisket

Sauce

1 cup peanut oil
1½ cups Accent
½ cup minced garlic
1 large container Creole sauce
½ cup onion flakes
6 chopped green onions (including stems), or
4 medium to large white onions, quartered
Vegetables or cooked rice
Whole red potatoes with skin
Corn on the cob

This hot and spicy meal is great for feeding a crowd and the cooking is traditionally done outdoors by the men. A Ralph family favorite first introduced by brother-in-law, Tony Swords, of Nachitoches, LA.

Fill a turkey fryer size stockpot ⅔ full of hot water. Add sauce ingredients. Bring to a boil. Add meat. Cover and boil for 4 to 5 hours, adding hot water as needed. Remove meat when tender. Add vegetables to stockpot. Boil until done. Remove. Reserve a quart of sauce to be poured over meat, vegetables and rice as desired.

Judith Ralph

Ralph's Best Backyard Barbecue Sauce

My mother-in-law, Ruby Ralph, first introduced me to the method of boiling meat before barbecuing for a tender and tantalizing dish. I always enjoyed Ruby's home-style cooking on the homeplace.

1 stick butter
1 cup catsup
½ cup vinegar
½ cup Worcestershire sauce
12-ounce bottle of hickory-flavored barbecue sauce
1 teaspoon hot sauce
1 can beer, optional
Salt and pepper to taste

Melt butter in a large saucepan. Add remaining ingredients, mix and simmer until well heated. Stir often.

Judith Ralph

"Andrew Jackson Ralph, better known to family as 'Grandpa Andy,' was one of those fishermen who enjoyed the challenge of scouring the banks of small creeks in Ohio County — looking to catch a fish with his not-so-common hook, the hand. Noodlers like Andy, I am told, plunge into a body of water, feeling along its bank for a hole of some sort, an old log, a rock crevice or possibly a mass of tree roots to run their hand up into until they find something. Once the noodler locates a fish, he tickles its belly, slowly inching his fingers toward the head. Then the skilled noodler slides a finger into the gill, hooking his supper."

Judith Ralph

Back Family Favorite Fried Fish

3 to 4 pounds crappie filet
2 cups self-rising cornmeal
2 teaspoons salt
½ teaspoon pepper
Dash of cayenne pepper
Vegetable oil

"How to cook carp. Skin the carp, take out the mud vein. Wash well in fresh water. Place on clean board, about 2x8 inches. After cleaning well, remove the carp and eat the board."

Filet the crappie and cut into small pieces. Combine the cornmeal, salt, pepper, and cayenne pepper. Roll the filets in the cornmeal mixture. Drop into the hot oil and fry until golden brown. Drain on paper towels.

Foy Back

Mamaw Punch's Hearty Hamburger Patties

1 pound ground beef
2 slices bread soaked in milk
2 teaspoons diced onion
Salt and Pepper to taste

Mix together thoroughly. Form into 4 individual patties. Fry in 1/2 stick of butter. Makes 4 servings.

Pamela Ralph Howard

"Sudi Oliver, being part Indian, knew how to catch a mess of fish. She made Dad his first fishing pole. She cut a willow switch from a tree in the backyard, attached a line, and then made a sinker from a Kentucky Long Rifle, percussion 38 caliber bullet. Next, she found a cork, probably a bottle stopper, and made a floater, before finishing the pole off by tying a hook to the end of the line."

"Grandmother Sudi and Dad went to a ditch that day and caught a large catch of fish. Dad recalls how proud he was as he carried the string of fish home to his mother, who to his surprise was too busy to fix them. Recognizing Dad's disappointment, Grandmother Sudi stepped in and said, 'Well, I'll cook them for you.' And she did. She grabbed up the string of fish, cut their heads off, rolled them in cornmeal, and then deep-fried them in a large kettle of melted lard. Dad describes that fishing trip with his grandmother as one of his fondest childhood memories."

Brenda Oliver Young

"Anything that grows under the ground, starts off in cold water - potatoes, beets, carrots, etc.

Anything that grows above the ground, starts off in boiling water - peas, green beans, etc."

Joyce Leach

Blue Ribbon Banana Pudding

1 stick butter
2 cups graham cracker crumbs, reserving ¼ cup
½ cup sugar
3½-ounce box vanilla instant pudding,
prepared according to directions
3½-ounce box banana instant pudding,
prepared according to directions
8-ounce package cream cheese
12-ounce tub non-dairy whipped topping
1 can sweetened condensed milk
6 bananas, sliced

This modern, yet deliciously rich and creamy version of banana pudding is a favorite of my daughter, Julie and her husband Jimmy.

Melt butter. Add graham cracker crumbs and sugar to the melted butter. Press into bottom of a 10½x14¾x2¼-inch pan. Mix puddings together, set aside. Blend cream cheese, whipped topping, and sweetened condensed milk; add pudding mixture, blend well. Layer ½ sliced bananas on crust. Pour ½ pudding mixture over bananas. Repeat layering. For a pretty topping, sprinkle reserved crumbs on top. Refrigerate. Best if sets overnight.

Judith Ralph

Michael's Tiny Cream Cheese Biscuits

The best indicator for a great recipe is my children. My son Michael devoured these the first time I made them, making them a permanent part of our recipe collection.

8-ounce package cream cheese, softened
½ cup butter or margarine, softened
1 cup self-rising flour

Beat cream cheese and butter at medium speed of an electric mixer for 2 minutes or until creamy. Gradually add flour, beating at low speed just until blended. Spoon dough into ungreased miniature (1¾-inch) muffin pans, filling full. Bake at 400 degrees for 15 minutes or until golden. Serve immediately. Makes 18 miniature biscuits.

Kim Mitchell

"Peppermint was used to help prevent or cure stomach cancer. It seemed to be the choice item for stomach ailments."

Brenda Oliver Young

Civil War Cake

3 medium-size apples, chopped
1 cup brown sugar
2 tablespoons shortening
2 cups raisins
1 cup granulated sugar
2 cups water
3 cups all-purpose flour
2 teaspoons soda
1 teaspoon cloves
1 teaspoon cinnamon
1 teaspoon salt

Combine first 6 ingredients in a saucepan and place over direct heat. After mixture begins to boil remove from heat. Cool. Mix together the dry ingredients. Add the cooled mixture to the flour mixture, beating well. Pour into a well greased and floured tube cake pan. Bake at 325 degrees for about 60 minutes.

Judy Back

"Rhubarb leaves are poisonous; cook only the stalk."

Hubert Oliver

My hus-band, Dennis, rates this cake as "the best" when using the handle of a wooden spoon to pierce large holes in the cake and saturating with a double recipe of glaze.

Lemon Lover's Cake

Cake

1 package lemon cake mix
3-ounce package lemon instant pudding mix
4 eggs
¼ cup oil
1 cup water

Glaze

6-ounce can frozen lemonade, thawed
1 cup confectioner's sugar

Combine cake mix, pudding mix, and eggs in a large bowl; mix well. Add the oil and water; beat until well blended. Pour into greased 9x13-inch cake pan. Bake at 350 degrees for 45 to 50 minutes or until cake tests done. Cool for 5 minutes. Combine lemonade and confectioner's sugar in bowl; beat until smooth. Pierce holes in cake with fork. Pour glaze over cake.

Judith Ralph

"We had a large chicken house in the back corner of our yard. I remember feeding the chickens at about dusk and bats would fly overhead sometimes. I was always scared of them. If you threw a corncob at them, they would kind of dive after it."

Emogene Miller Moseley

Hot Fudge Sundae Cake

✶ If using self-rising flour, omit baking powder and salt.

1 cup all-purpose flour*
¾ cup granulated sugar
¼ cup plus 2 tablespoons cocoa, divided
2 teaspoons baking powder
¼ teaspoon salt
½ cup milk
2 tablespoons vegetable oil
1 teaspoon vanilla
1 cup chopped nuts, if desired
1 cup packed brown sugar
1¾ cups hottest tap water
Ice Cream

Heat oven to 350 degrees. Mix flour, granulated sugar, 2 tablespoons cocoa, baking powder and salt in ungreased square pan, 9x9x2 inches. Mix in milk, oil and vanilla with fork until smooth. Stir in nuts. Spread in pan. Sprinkle with brown sugar and ¼ cup cocoa. Pour hot water over batter. Bake 40 minutes. Serve warm, topped with ice cream. spoon sauce from pan onto each serving.

Kim Mitchell

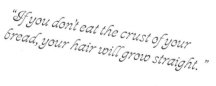

"If you don't eat the crust of your bread, your hair will grow straight."

Tom Schultz

I remember the first time I tasted this wonderful dessert. A southern friend served it while still warm. I was so glad when I came across the recipe years later. My family enjoys this as one of their favorite pies. It always brings my son Daniel to the kitchen when he smells it baking.

Warm Your Heart Buttermilk Pie

½ cup butter or margarine, softened
2 cups sugar
3 tablespoons all-purpose flour
3 eggs
1 cup buttermilk
1 teaspoon vanilla extract
One unbaked 9-inch pastry shell

Cream butter at high speed of an electric mixer; gradually add sugar, beating well. Add flour, and beat until smooth. Add eggs; beat until blended. Add buttermilk and vanilla, beat well. Pour filling into pastry shell. Bake at 400 degrees for 5 minutes; reduce heat to 350 degrees, and bake an additional 45 minutes or until set. Cool to room temperature; then chill. Makes one 9-inch pie.

Kim Mitchell

Buttermilk Substitute

1 cup sweet milk
2 tablespoons vinegar

Add vinegar to sweet milk. Let stand a few minutes. Use as needed in recipe.

Judith Ralph

Sugar-Free Banana Pie

3-ounce package sugar-free vanilla instant pudding
1 cup sour cream
12-ounce tub whipped topping
3 bananas
1 graham cracker crust
½ cup chopped pecans, optional

Stir together pudding mix, sour cream, and whipped topping, blending well. Slice the bananas into bottom of crust. Pour pudding mix over the bananas. Sprinkle chopped pecans over top, if desired.

Joyce Leach

"When I was a child, you had to doctor yourself. Kerosene was poured straight on sores to make wounds heal and turpentine dropped into a teaspoonful of sugar was given as treatment for a sore throat."

Hubert Oliver

July

A season of steadfastness

"Whom resist steadfast in the faith…God…after that ye have suffered a while, make you perfect, establish, strengthen, settle you."

1 Peter 5: 9,10

Ralph Mitchell, Daniel Mitchell, Tom Schultz, Michael Mitchell

"Long Row to Hoe"

As a child growing up on the farm,
Life was sometimes rough.
We ate our breakfast before daylight,
And worked all day till dusk.
I hoed a million rows of corn,
That seemed to have no end.
Then with a drink of water,
I would start back out again.
I looked up ever' now and then,
Praying for a cloud.
If it started raining we would head
Out for the house.
I thought someday I will find a way
To leave this farm for good;
Then I won't have to hoe the corn
And carry in the wood.
Years flew by and times were hard,
After I moved away.
I worked from sunrise until dark,
Almost everyday.
I thought, some day I will find a way
To leave this place for good.
I'll go back home and hoe the corn
And carry in the wood.
I'll leave this dirty city with
Its trouble and its strife,
For the years I spent down on the farm,
Were the best years of my life.

Kathryn Bailey

Lori's Chicken Salad

4 or 5 boneless chicken breasts, fried thoroughly in oil
½ cup real mayonnaise
¼ cup diced celery
1 cup sliced red grapes
1 cup sliced almonds, toasted lightly in oven
Juice from ½ lemon
Lemon pepper to taste

Drain and cool cooked chicken. Chop finely. Mix with remaining ingredients. Chill before serving.

Lori Harris

Just Right Chicken Salad

4 chicken breasts
1 small onion, chopped
½ cup pickle cubes
2 stalks celery, finely chopped
½ cup nuts, chopped
¾ cup salad dressing
1 tablespoon prepared mustard
1 heaping tablespoon sugar
¼ cup cream
1 teaspoon vinegar

Boil chicken breast, let cool. Chop in small pieces. Add next four ingredients. Mix together salad dressing, mustard, sugar, cream, and vinegar until smooth. Pour over the chicken. Stir well. Enjoy!

Judy Back

Batter Dipped Frog Legs

1 egg, beaten
½ teaspoon salt
½ cup cornmeal or flour
⅛ teaspoon pepper
2 pounds frog legs
½ cup cooking oil

Mix the egg, salt, cornmeal, and pepper together to form a batter. Dip frog legs in batter. Fry in hot oil in a large iron skillet for about 25 minutes, turning as needed.

Judith Ralph

Fried Green Tomatoes

4 large green tomatoes, sliced
1 cup self-rising flour
¼ cup sugar
½ cup oil

Cover tomatoes in ice water and soak for 15 minutes. Drain. Sift flour and sugar into shallow dish. Coat tomatoes well, fry in hot oil in skillet until golden brown, about 2½ minutes per side.

Judith Ralph

Depression Cake

3 cups all-purpose flour
2 cups sugar
1 teaspoon salt
2 teaspoons baking soda
⅓ cup cocoa
3 teaspoons vanilla
6 tablespoons vinegar
¾ cup vegetable oil
2 cups water

Mix all ingredients well. Pour into greased 9x13 pan. Bake at 350 degrees for 30 to 40 minutes.

Willa M. Spradling

"Mamaw Punch said the secret to a moist box cake is to add extra shortening and do not over cook."

Pamela Ralph Howard

White Texas Sheet Cake

Barry made this cake and I thought it was one of the most delicious cakes that I had ever eaten. The almond extract gives it a unique flavor.

1 cup margarine
1 cup water
2 cups all-purpose flour
2 cups sugar
2 eggs, beaten
½ cup sour cream
1 teaspoon almond extract
1 teaspoon salt
1 teaspoon baking soda

In a large saucepan bring margarine and water to a boil. Remove from heat; stir in flour, sugar, eggs, sour cream, almond extract, salt and baking soda until smooth. Pour into a greased 9x13 baking pan. Bake at 375 degrees for 20 to 22 minutes, or until cake tests done. Cool 20 minutes, then add frosting.

Frosting

½ cup margarine
½ cup milk
4½ cups powdered sugar
½ teaspoon almond extract
1 cup chopped walnuts

While cake is cooling, combine margarine and milk in saucepan. Bring to a boil. Remove from heat and add sugar and almond extract and mix well. Stir in walnuts and spread over warm cake.

Emogene Moseley

Mom's Blackberry Cobbler

4 cups blackberries
¾ cup granulated sugar
1 stick butter
1 cup self-rising flour
1 cup sugar
1 cup milk

Combine blackberries and sugar in saucepan. Add just enough water to cover berries. Cook until softened. Melt butter in 9x13 pan. Mix together flour, sugar, and milk. Pour over margarine. Pour berries and juice on top. Bake until crust rises to the top and is browned.

Kathryn Bailey

"On Christmas Eve, we left hay in the stable for Santa's reindeer. In the morning, the hay was gone."

Charles Curtis Moseley

Two Nannie's Blackberry Batty Cakes

Double biscuit dough recipe
1 quart blackberries
Sugar to taste
Butter
Sugar and cinnamon, mixed together
Whipped cream or ice cream

Make a double batch of biscuit dough. Divide dough and pat into the size of your crock (2 or 3 to a cookie sheet). Bake as you would for biscuits. Let them cool, cut horizontally. Put the round top in the bottom of a crock or a deep oven safe bowl. On top of the stove combine blackberries and sugar. Cook until blackberries are tender. Pour a portion over the batty cake half. Add pinches of butter. Put on the next half of batty cake. Repeat process ending with blackberries and butter. On top, sprinkle a little sugar mixed with cinnamon so it makes a crunchy top. Serve with whipped cream or ice cream.

Linda Brothers

Two Nannie is a name I gave my grandmother on my father's side. My mother's mother was Grannie and my father's mother was Two Nannie because she was my 2nd grannie. She would set this recipe in her warming oven, on top of her wood stove, so it was served warm.

"I always hid behind my paper lunch sack to eat my biscuits and jam at school. Back then it was a disgrace to have biscuits for lunch. The children from families with money had light bread for their sandwiches.'"

Anna Mary Leach

Banana Split Dessert

Crust

2 cups graham cracker crumbs
6 tablespoons margarine

Mix together and pat into bottom of a 9x13 pan. Bake 10 minutes at 350 degrees.

2 eggs
1 stick margarine
2 cups powdered sugar
1 teaspoon vanilla
3 or 4 bananas
20-ounce can crushed pineapple, drained
1 quart whipped topping
½ cup chopped nuts
1 cup chopped maraschino cherries

Blend eggs, margarine, powdered sugar and vanilla until fluffy; spread over crust. Then slice bananas and put on mixture. On this, spread crushed pineapple. Top with whipped topping. Sprinkle top with chopped nuts and maraschino cherries. Refrigerate 6 hours or overnight.

Phyllis Blanton

Cherry Torte

16 crushed graham crackers
½ cup melted butter
¾ cup sugar, divided
8-ounce package softened cream cheese
2 eggs
1 can cherry pie filling
Whipped topping, optional

This is my oldest and favorite dessert recipe.

Mix graham crackers, melted butter, and ¼ cup sugar together. Press into 8x8 pan. In another bowl beat together cream cheese, ½ cup sugar, and eggs. Pour mixture over graham cracker mix and bake at 350 degrees for 35 minutes. Chill. Top with cherry pie filling. Add whipped topping, if desired.

Jerl Dean Adkins

"Tie a dirty wool sock around your neck for a sore throat - the dirtier the better!"

Ruby Ralph

The Best Homemade Vanilla Ice Cream

5 eggs
3½ cups sugar
1 can evaporated milk
2½ quarts whole milk
1 tablespoon vanilla extract
5-quart ice cream freezer

Beat eggs in a large mixing bowl until well beaten. Gradually add sugar to eggs and continue beating until well blended and creamy. Beat in evaporated milk until well blended. Then add vanilla extract and milk. Stir well. Make in ice cream freezer, according to freezer directions.

Emogene Moseley

"*This was a recipe of my mother's. In the 1950s, I remember the men taking turns on hot Sunday afternoons turning the handle on the crank type freezer with a grass sack over the top of the freezer to keep the cold air inside so the ice cream would freeze quicker. They always made it on our gravel driveway, so the salt water would not kill the grass in our yard. It did not take long to dish it all out after waiting about 30 minutes for it to freeze. It has become as much of a tradition in my family to have this homemade ice cream on our birthdays as it is to have a birthday cake. Of course, I now use an electric ice cream freezer.*"

August

A season of understanding

*"Through wisdom is an house builded; and by
understanding it is established."*
Proverbs 24:3

Estil, Foy, Shirl, Merle, Redge, Randy, Denzil and Nila Blair Back

"When Mama was 41 years old, she came down with inflammatory rheumatism. It was in the summer. She couldn't move and had to stay in bed for 18 weeks. We poured boiling water into stone crocks and wrapped them in cloth. We placed 3 on each side of her body. We wrapped hot irons and laid them against her feet. We couldn't touch Mama because it was too painful for her. I was 11 years old and had to get up in the mornings before school to cook breakfast. I had to cook and clean after school. I had to do the family washing on a washboard. Mama told me to boil the clothes outside in a big long wash kettle, heated over a natural gas fire. Mama said the boiling would remove a lot of dirt. Mama was in bed the entire summer."

Anna Mary Leach

"We used to milk 11 cows every morning before school. One old cow filled a No. 2 wash tub to the brim with fresh milk."

Dennis Ralph

Soap

Use cast iron, stainless steel or porcelain kettle. Do not use an aluminum pot.

32 ounces cold water
1 can lye
9 ounces castor oil
22 ounces olive oil
22 ounces coconut oil
2 pounds melted lard

Using a wooden spoon, mix cold water and can of lye together. Stir until lye is dissolved and cool. Mix in the oils and melted lard. Stir until the thickness of honey. Pour into a glass dish or cardboard box lined with a cloth. When firm, cut into cakes.

Laundry Soap

1 can lye
½ cup Clorox
¾ cup 20 Mule Team Borax
3 quarts minus 5 tablespoons cold water
9 cups grease, #2 coffee can

Dissolve lye in water in an enamel pan or iron kettle. Stir together Clorox and borax until dissolved. Add to the lye water. Pour into grease. Stir continually for 15 minutes. Pour into prepared pan or box. Set aside and cut when set.

Willa M. Spradling

King Ranch Chicken Casserole

1 large onion, chopped
1 large green bell pepper, chopped
2 garlic cloves, minced
2 tablespoons vegetable oil
2 cups chopped cooked chicken
10¾-ounce can cream of chicken soup, undiluted
10¾-ounce can cream of mushroom soup, undiluted
10-ounce can diced tomato and green chiles, undrained
1 teaspoon chili powder
¼ teaspoon pepper
Twelve 6-inch corn tortillas
1½ cups Monterey Jack cheese
1½ cups cheddar cheese

Sauté onion, bell pepper, and garlic in hot oil in a large skillet over medium-high heat 5 minutes or until tender. Remove from heat; stir in chicken and next 5 ingredients. Tear corn tortillas into pieces; layer one-third of tortilla pieces in a lightly-greased 9x13 baking dish. Top with one-third of chicken mixture and one-third of mixed cheese. Repeat layers twice. Cover and bake at 350 degrees for 25 minutes. Uncover and bake 5 more minutes or until bubbly. Makes 6 to 8 servings.

Kim Mitchell

Stuffed Green Peppers in Crock Pot

5 to 6 green peppers
1 pound ground beef
½ cup instant rice
1¼ teaspoons salt
¼ teaspoon pepper
1 egg, slightly beaten
¼ cup milk
1 small onion, finely chopped
26-ounce can tomato soup
1 soup can water

Remove core and seeds from peppers and wash peppers. Combine ground beef, rice, salt, pepper, egg, milk and onion. Stuff peppers lightly and place in crock pot. Pour tomato soup and water over stuffed peppers. Cook on high about 8 hours.

Emogene Moseley

"Me and my brother Arthur would dig coal out of the branch to burn in the winter. Was lots of coal, about four or five inches thick."

Clarence Miller

Best Baked Beans

Two 16 to 18-ounce cans pork and beans
¾ cup brown sugar
1 teaspoon dry mustard
½ cup catsup
6 slices bacon, cooked, drained, and crumbled

Mix pork and beans, brown sugar, dry mustard, and catsup. Add bacon. Pour into dish greased with bacon drippings. Bake 325 degrees for 2½ hours, uncovered.

Jerl Dean Adkins

Creek Fries

7 large potatoes, sliced
5 teaspoons butter
Salt and pepper to taste
1½ cups Velveeta cheese, shredded
6 slices bacon, crisply fried and drained

Place sliced potatoes on a large sheet of heavy weight aluminum foil. Dot with butter. Add seasonings. Wrap, seal, then place on top rack of grill over medium heat. Cook for 1 hour, or until tender. Remove from heat. Cover with cheese. Crumble bacon slices over the cheese. Rewrap and return to grill until cheese melts.

Julie Ralph Alford

Home-Style Macaroni and Cheese

8 ounces macaroni
1-inch slab of American cheese, cubed
¾ cup milk
¼ cup butter

Cook macaroni, drain. Return to low heat. Stir in cheese, milk, and butter until creamy.

Julie Ralph Alford

Overnight Salad

1 head lettuce, shredded
1 head cauliflower flowerettes
1 purple onion, sliced
1 pound bacon
¼ cup sugar
⅓ cup Parmesan cheese
½ cup real mayonnaise
Salt and pepper

Layer first 4 ingredients starting with lettuce. Sprinkle with sugar and salt and pepper. Add Parmesan cheese. Top with mayonnaise, covering side to side. Toss lightly.

Kathryn Mitchell

Mama Comley's Pepper Relish

2 dozen ground green peppers
1 dozen ground onions
3 cups sugar
1 quart vinegar

Put peppers in pan and scald for 5 minutes. Drain through colander and rinse several times. Add onions, sugar and vinegar. Heat to boiling point. Put into pint jars. Makes 7 pints.

Kathryn Mitchell

Sour Cream Loaves

¼ pound margarine, creamed
1 cup granulated sugar
2 eggs, whole
8-ounce container sour cream
2 teaspoons vanilla
2 cups flour
1 teaspoon baking soda
2 tablespoons flour
3 tablespoons sugar
2 tablespoons cinnamon

Grease and flour 2 loaf pans. Combine all the ingredients except flour, sugar, and cinnamon. Pour half the batter into the pan. Mix together flour, sugar, and cinnamon for topping. Sprinkle ¾ of the topping onto the batter. Pour in remaining batter. Top with remaining topping. Bake at 350 degrees for 45 minutes. Makes 2 loaves.

Kathryn Mitchell

My Granny

"Kathryn Mitchell is my awesome Granny. She wears glasses, but I still can see her beautiful blue eyes. She is always wearing a light blue sweater. Every time I think of her I picture her in that sweater. She has a favorite chair and every time she sits down is usually in that chair. But what she does most of all is smile. Whenever she smiles, it reminds me of how much fun we always have."

"My Granny is the one who is teaching me how to cook. We always have fun when we cook. I remember when we made banana bread. First, we got all the ingredients out. Then we mixed it all in a big bowl. We stirred it up real good. We weren't laughing but we were having lots of fun because we were spending time together. We poured the mix into the pan and popped it into the oven. Pretty soon we smelled a delicious smell. We took the bread out of the oven and cut us each a slice. It tasted fabulous! I have gained more confidence about cooking from my Granny."

Katie Browning

"Myrtle would visit us on the farm in Ohio County on the holidays. Every 4th of July, she and her husband, Leamon, would come driping up in their Franklin auto-mobile with a 50-pound block of ice tied to the front. We made homemade ice cream in a lard can by first, filling the can with our ice cream mixture, then turning it in a wash-tub of crushed ice. She also treated us to gingerale."

Anna Mary Leach

White Chocolate Cheese Cake

Two 8-ounce packages cream cheese, softened
½ cup sugar
½ teaspoon vanilla
2 eggs, beaten
4 squares white chocolate, or ⅔ cup white chocolate chips
1 prepared crust (Oreo, graham, or cookie)

Mix cream cheese, sugar and vanilla with electric mixer until well blended. Add eggs and melted white chocolate squares. Pour into crust of choice. Bake at 350 degrees for 35 minutes until done. Refrigerate 3 hours or overnight.

Debra Richards

"Our son Barry was born in 1962. I remember seeing the news of the Cuban Missile Crisis on TV in the hospital after he was born. This was a period of time when everyone thought Russia might drop an atom bomb on the U.S. We had dug a basement under our house and thought about building a bomb shelter in it, but never did. The government was holding meetings and giving out pamphlets with instructions on how to build the shelter, how long to stay in it to avoid radiation, and food and supplies to have stored in it."

Emogene Miller Moseley

Fresh Peach Dessert

1 bag Pecan Sandies Cookies
1 stick melted margarine
8-ounce package cream cheese, at room temperature
1 cup powdered sugar
8-ounce carton whipped topping
10-ounce bottle 7-UP
4 tablespoons cornstarch
1 cup sugar
3 tablespoons peach gelatin
6 to 8 medium peaches, sliced

Crush cookies, add melted margarine. Press in 9x13-inch pan. Bake crust at 325 degrees for 10 minutes. Mix cream cheese, powdered sugar and whipped topping. Spread over cool crust. Bring 7-UP, cornstarch, sugar, and gelatin to a boil. Boil 3 to 4 minutes, and then cool. Add sliced peaches. Pour over cream cheese mixture and chill.

Emogene Moseley

"Our family made a bitter herbal tea from boiling boneset. It was used for a variety of medicinal purposes."

Hubert Oliver

The sauce that you pour over this cobbler is a recipe from my mother-in-law, Ester Moseley. I had never eaten a cobbler with sauce like this until I had it at the Moseley farm. I made this cobbler and sauce for Charles to take to work when they had special meals. His co-workers have often told me how delicious the cobbler was when we met up with them at retirement dinners and such.

Windy Hill Blackberry Cobbler and Sauce

Cobbler Crust

2¼ cups self-rising flour
⅓ cup oil
⅔ cup milk

Stir flour, oil, and milk to make soft ball of dough. Flour a flat surface and knead dough. Then roll dough out big enough to fit into a 9x12x2 pan with enough dough left on the sides to fold over the top of the blackberry mixture. Press into a greased pan.

Blackberry Filling

1 cup sugar
Two 16½-ounce cans blackberries in water
½ stick margarine
3 tablespoons sugar

Stir sugar in bowl with blackberries. Pour over crust in pan. Fold sides of crust over blackberry mixture to form crust for top of cobbler. Dot top of crust with margarine. Sprinkle sugar over top of margarine and crust. Bake in 400-degree oven 45 to 55 minutes.

Sauce

¾ cup sugar
¼ cup flour
Dash of salt
3 cups water
⅓ cup margarine
1 teaspoon vanilla extract

Stir sugar, flour, and salt in saucepan. Add water and margarine. Boil over medium heat, stirring constantly, until it strikes a boil. Continue stirring at a low boil for about 2 minutes. Add vanilla. Pour in bowl and serve as a sauce to pour over cobbler, if desired.

Emogene Moseley

"Boil the fat off a rabbit's kidney until the kidney becomes spongy. Pack fat from kidney in ear for an earache."

Debra Richards

Pig Pickin' Cake

1 box butter recipe yellow cake mix
½ cup vegetable oil
4 eggs
11-ounce can mandarin oranges, undrained
20-ounce can crushed pineapple, undrained
2 cups milk
5-ounce box instant vanilla pudding
8-ounce package cream cheese
16-ounce bowl whipped topping
Coconut

Mix cake mix, oil, eggs, oranges and juice with mixer. Bake in greased 9x13-inch pan 35 to 40 minutes at 350 degrees. While cake is warm, make holes in top with end of wooden spoon. Pour pineapple over it. Mix milk with pudding mix. Add cream cheese and mix well. Spread over cake. Spread whipped topping over pudding mixture. Sprinkle with coconut.

Kim Mitchell

"Dip a string in kerosene then tie it around your table legs to prepent ants from climbing onto the table."

Clarence Miller

September

A season of revisiting

"…He shall return to the days of his youth."
Job 33:25

Redge Back and Foy Back

Reunion Day

I remember that first reunion day
When Granny was old and I was young;
How sweet September wore her veil of grey,
With the breath of autumn upon her face.

How we gathered together before the Lord,'
Our little family, so humble and fine,
'Round a banquet table, mere rows of board,
Upon which laid end summer garden's bountiful hoard.

How fireflies danced above the earth,
And children laughed at stories told;
How life was restored once more to Mom's place of birth,
Measured not by riches and gold was its worth.

Long since that first reunion day
When Granny was old and I was young,
Life's grand finale has called many away,
Then replaced its cry with that of a newborn babe.

Judith Moseley Ralph

Picnic-Style Ham

One 8 to10 pound ham
2 cups water
1 teaspoon dry mustard
1 teaspoon whole cloves
3 tablespoons vinegar
1 cup brown sugar

Boil ham in large pot of water for 1 hour. Drain. Add 2 cups water, mustard, cloves, vinegar, and brown sugar. Bring to a boil and boil slowly for 1 hour, turning the ham after 30 minutes. Slice and eat.

Joyce Leach

Crispy Fried Squirrel

Clean squirrel thoroughly, disjoint it, cut the back into two pieces. Put in large glass container with salt water and soak overnight in refrigerator. Next morning, drain and dry pieces and remove any loose membrane. Roll in seasoned flour. Heat oil or lard (do not use vegetable shortening) in heavy skillet. Brown the pieces, turning once. Cover skillet, cook about 30 minutes longer. Remove meat from skillet, pour off all but 3 tablespoons fat. Add 2 tablespoons seasoned flour. When flour is brown, stir in equal parts milk and water and cook, stirring until thick. Serve with homemade biscuits.

James Lexter Leach

"One time when I was squirrel hunting, I came upon the neighbor man running a batch of moonshine. He took off running until he saw that it was me and Pap. When the moonshine dripped from the copper coil on the still, it ran clear. Burnt brown sugar was added to give it the amber color."

Cheesiest Scalloped Potatoes Ever

6 medium potatoes, peeled and sliced
1 teaspoon salt
1 tablespoon flour
10 slices American cheese
½ cup butter
3 cups milk

Butter 2½-quart baking dish. Layer half each of potatoes, salt, flour, and cheese, dot with ¼ cup butter. Repeat layers. Fill with milk to top of potatoes. Bake at 375 degrees covered, until starts to bubble. Remove lid and continue to bake until potatoes are tender; approximately 1½ hours baking time.

Emogene Miller Moseley

"When my brother and I were young, Dad would often decide to take a Sunday afternoon drive to Rough River Dam State Park. Mom always packed a picnic lunch, usually ham or fried chicken, baked beans, and the cheesiest scalloped potatoes ever."

Judith Ralph

Widow Wagon Salad

8-ounce carton cottage cheese
3½-ounce box of strawberry gelatin
11-ounce can crushed pineapple
11-ounce can mandarin oranges
8-ounce tub whipped topping

Mix cottage cheese and gelatin. Drain fruit and add to mixture. Add whipped topping. Let sit until slightly firm.

Mandy Perkins Wright

My great-grandmother never missed a church dinner. She always took this dessert when the "widow wagon" (church van) came to pick her up.

"My mama and my daddy had 13 kids, and we lived on a farm. I had 12 brothers and sisters, imagine that! We only went to the store to buy things that my mama couldn't make, like toilet paper and detergent. If we couldn't raise it on the farm, we didn't eat it. We got our milk from the Holstein and our eggs from the chickens."

"We didn't have a bathroom, a toilet, or a tub. We heated our bath water on the stove. We didn't have toys. We made mud pies and corn shuck dolls. I remember twisting the dried blade into little heads with my fingers…"

"When I look back, I thought that I was miserable, but now I know that those were the best days of my life. Now I know that happiness doesn't come from what you have, it comes from inside, from what you hold in your heart."

Rita Robinson

Honest to Goodness Homemade Bread

3 cups warm milk, I use dry milk powder and water to
make 3 cups milk
1½ teaspoons salt
½ cup sugar
½ cup shortening, I use bacon fat
2 tablespoons yeast, or 2 packages
About 9 cups bread flour

Thoroughly mix all ingredients, turn out onto floured board
and knead until smooth and satiny, about 10 minutes. Place
in greased bowl, grease top of bread dough. Let rise in warm
place, until double in size, about 1 hour. Then divide dough
into 3 loaves. Place in greased 9x5-inch pans. Let rise to top
of pans. Bake at 400 degrees for 30 minutes. I use this
dough for cinnamon rolls, too.

Willa M. Spradling

*"Bill, as anyone who knows Willa, refers to her as, is
well known in the community for her healing insights,
beautiful homemade quilts, and delicious homemade bread.
My nieces and I visited Bill back in the summer and were met
with hot, out of the oven, homemade bread. Before she served
us she smothered the steamy hot bread with a stick of butter. It
put a whole new twist on the phrase, 'finger lick'n good.'"*

Kim Mitchell

Corn Bread Muffins

1 cup self-rising cornmeal
2 eggs, beaten
½ cup vegetable oil
1 cup sour cream
1 cup cream-style corn

Combine cornmeal, eggs, oil, sour cream, and corn in bowl. Mix well. Pour into greased muffin cups. Bake at 450 degrees for 15 to 20 minutes, or until brown. Makes 16 muffins.

Judith Ralph

"My grandmother, Martha Jane Hale, made a black salve, an ointment that was said to have cured boils on the skin."

Clarence Miller

Old-Time Apple Stack Cake

½ cup butter
½ cup brown sugar
½ cup sorghum
2 eggs
⅔ cup buttermilk
1 level teaspoon baking soda
3½ cups all-purpose flour
¼ level teaspoon ground cloves
¼ teaspoon cinnamon
¼ teaspoon nutmeg
Dried apples, soaked over night

Cream butter and sugar; add sorghum, eggs, and buttermilk mixed with soda; then add sifted flour and spices. Place sufficient batter for each layer on well-floured board, knead lightly and roll as a pie crust (¼-inch thick). Measure with tea plate. Bake in greased skillet or round cake tins, 15 minutes in 375 degree oven. Soak dried apples overnight, then cook until done. Flavor to taste with brown sugar and ground cloves. Stack cakes with apple filling between each layer and on top. Put together while both are hot. If no dried apples are available, use applesauce flavored as directed. Do not cut for 24 hours. This is a very old mountain recipe.

Martha Motley

"When Mama sliced apples for drying, it was my job to climb up to the top of the porch roof and lay them out. We dried both peaches and apples that way."

Norman Matthews

Harvest Spice Apple Crisp

4 cups raw apples, peeled and sliced
½ cup water
¾ cup flour
1 cup brown sugar
¼ teaspoon salt
1 teaspoon cinnamon
½ cup butter, melted

Butter bottom of baking dish. Place apples and water in baking dish. In a separate mixing bowl mix flour, brown sugar, salt, cinnamon, and melted butter with a fork. Spread evenly over apples and bake at 350 degrees until apples are tender and brown approximately 30 minutes.

Kim Mitchell

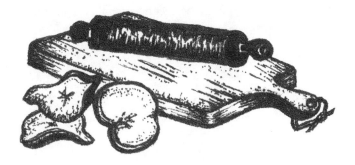

JVR '02

Orange Dreamsicle Cake

1 box orange cake mix
3-ounce box orange gelatin
⅓ cup cooking oil
1¼ cups water
3 eggs
1 teaspoon orange extract

Preheat oven to 350 degrees. Grease and flour two 9-inch cake pans and set aside. Blend all ingredients and pour into cake pans. Bake about 25 minutes.

Icing

8 ounces sour cream
12-ounce package shredded coconut, optional
1¼ cups granulated sugar
½ cup frozen orange juice concentrate, thawed
8-ounce container whipped topping

After cake layers cool, slice each layer in half to make 4 layers. Combine sour cream and coconut. Blend sugar and orange juice in another mixing bowl, until sugar dissolves. Combine juice mixture and coconut mixture. Fold in whipped topping. Spread between cake layers and on top and sides. Keep refrigerated.

Emogene Miller Moseley

Delightfully Delicious Date Nut Cookies

This recipe was given a triple thumbs up by the Zion Baptist Church Ladies Bible Study Group.

¼ teaspoon salt
3 egg whites
1¼ cups confectioner's sugar
1 tablespoon flour
2 cups broken pecans
1 cup chopped dates
1 teaspoon vanilla

Add salt to egg whites, beat stiff. Sift the sugar with the flour. Add flour mixture to the beaten egg whites one tablespoon at a time. Keep beating until stiff. Fold in nuts, dates, and vanilla. Drop by small teaspoonfuls onto cookie sheet that is covered with aluminum foil and sprayed well with a cooking spray. Bake at 300 degrees for 20 to 30 minutes. Makes about 24 small cookies.

Kathryn Mitchell

"A poultice made from boiled peach tree leaves mixed with cornmeal was applied to sores to draw out infection. Once, when I had a thorn embedded in my flesh, a peach tree leaf poultice was wrapped around my foot, drawing out the thorn, as well as the infection."

Hubert Oliver

"As far back as I can remember, which is about 62 years, my grandparents and parents depended on herbs for all kinds of ailments. They headed for the woods in the spring and summer to dig for Goldenseal (yellow root), which was used for stomach ulcers, bladder infections, cold and flu and just about every ailment."

"They made a tea from the dried roots (which tasted terrible). I guess they figured what don't kill you will make you stronger."

"They usually had canned blackberries in the cellar; we got the juice for diarrhea and a blackberry cobbler sure tasted good in the winter time."

"Mother made cough syrups from green mullin leaves and pine needle. She sometimes added mountain tea leaves for the wintergreen flavor. She added sugar and water, boiled it into a syrup, then strained it. (Very tasty!)"

All from Kathryn Bailey

"I always loved the holidays when I was a child. The first Easter I recall was when we got an Easter basket with brightly-colored marshmallow eggs packed inside. I remember how pretty those bright red, green, yellow, purple, pink and orange eggs were. I never ate any of my candy. I saved it for months."

Emogene Miller Moseley

Ida Goodpastor's 100-Year-Old Chocolate Cake Recipe

First Part

2 cups sugar
¾ cup butter or lard mixture
2 eggs
1 teaspoon vanilla

Second Part

2 cups buttermilk or clabber milk
2 level tablespoons cocoa

add to first part
3½ cups all-purpose flour

Bake at 350 degrees for 25 minutes.

I like clabber milk better than buttermilk for this cake. You can use either one.

Sheila Isaac

120

October

A season of harvest

"And let us not be weary in well doing;
for in due season we shall reap; if we faint not."
Galatians 6:9

James Andrew and Allie Ralph

"*I spent a lot of time on the farm with Grandma, Grandpa and Aunt Lizzie and it was wonderful. We had sheep, cows, pigs, chickens, ducks, geese, guinea hens, mules for work and a horse to pull the buggy. There was work to do, as the farm was pretty well self-supporting. There was a large apple orchard, big garden and wood lot. Everyone entered into the operation of the farm, in the canning, preserving of food, each in its season. The geese were picked for their feathers and down, the sheep sheared and the wool made into clothing. We were able to sleep on feather beds while less well off folks often slept on mattresses made of straw.*"

Excerpt from "Something of the Moseley Family," written by and given to me by my great-uncle, the late William Todd Moseley.

Judith Ralph

"*Mam always purchased fresh straw for our bedding as winter approached. One year, money was so scarce, she sent us children out to cut dead grass after the first frost for our ticking.*"

James Lexter Leach

Cassoulet

This particular recipe was shared with me by a Western Kentucky friend while we were both living in North Carolina. It has truly become one of our family favorites, especially delicious when the temperature is cold outside.

½ pound bulk pork sausage
1 small onion, sliced (½ cup)
1 clove garlic, minced
½ pound (1½ cups) cubed cooked ham
2 tablespoons snipped parsley
1 bay leaf
Two 15-ounce cans navy beans
(or 2 cups dry beans, cooked)

Brown sausage, onion, and garlic. Drain grease. Add ham, parsley, and bay leaf. Stir in undrained beans. Pour into a 1½-quart casserole. Bake, covered, in 325 degrees oven for 45 minutes. Uncover, and bake 40 to 45 minutes more, stirring occasionally. Remove bay leaf. Makes 6 servings.

Kim Mitchell

"*My brother Steve and Uncle Denzil remember a true story about my Papaw Estil Back.
It was back when the state was trying to bring Cave Run Lake into the area. Papaw had some prime land and the 'big guys' wanted to buy it. They offered Papaw a price. He refused it. They decided to add a little more pressure, so they showed up at his house one day. He, of course, was at the barn stripping tobacco. Word was sent that he had company at the house. He sent word back that if they wanted to talk to him to come to the barn. The men began pressuring Papaw to sell and finally threatened to take him to court. Papaw welcomed the challenge and replied with, 'Alright, I haven't lost a court case yet.' The men turned around and walked away. Little did they know that Papaw hadn't lost a court case because he had never been to court. Papaw always said, 'Buy all the land you can, 'cause they're not making anymore.'*"

Kim Mitchell

Corn Fritters

1¾ cups all-purpose flour
2 teaspoons baking powder
¾ teaspoon salt
¾ cup milk
1 cup drained canned corn or grated fresh corn
1 egg, beaten
1 tablespoon melted fat

Mix together dry ingredients. Mix milk, corn, egg, and fat; add to dry ingredients, mixing well. Fry like a pancake in a small amount of oil. Serve with syrup. Makes about 12 fritters.

Linda Brothers

A Memory

Dad's Homemade Hominy

"*We shelled a lot of corn, which was put in a big iron kettle. He made a circle of rocks, built a fire, set the kettle on and we kept the fire going for hours. He added lye, don't know how much, the lye ate the husk off. We skimmed, washed and stirred. It seemed like forever, but it was worth all the work.*"

Parched Corn

"*We also made parched corn, love to have some right now. We put shelled corn in an iron skillet with just a little bacon grease, set it on the stove and stirred it (to keep from burning) until it was crisp and golden brown. Sure tasted better than fritos.*"

Kathryn Bailey

How to Make Hominy

1 gallon of shucked corn, yellow or white
2 tablespoons lye
Fresh water

Take corn and lye and place in a porcelain pot. Cover with water and boil until the husks begin to skin off. Remove from the fire and wash thoroughly with several washings until the husks skin is off. Put corn back in the kettle and cover with clean water. Bring back to boiling. Pour off water. Add fresh water and bring to boil again. This takes the strength of the lye out. Drain the water and cover once again with clean water, continue to cook until hominy is tender.

Kim Mitchell

"Grandpa Bill loved his grand-kids. No matter how many of us piled up in his lap, he always had room for one more."

Andrew Ralph

Mamaw's Basic Custard Pie

1¼ cups sugar
⅔ teaspoon salt
4 tablespoons cornstarch
2 heaping tablespoons flour
4 egg yolks
4½ cups milk
½ cup butter
2 teaspoons vanilla extract
2 baked pie shells

Mix sugar, salt, cornstarch, and flour together in a large saucepan. Beat egg yolks and milk together in a separate bowl, then slowly stir into dry mixture. Cook over medium heat, stirring continuously until mixture comes to a boil, then thickens, usually 1 to 2 minutes. Remove from heat then add butter and vanilla extract. Pour into baked pie shells and top with meringue.

Mamaw and Papaw raised 7 sons, most of which learned to cook as well as tend to the farm. The boys were especially fond of homemade custard pies made in a variety of ways. The main ingredients of the basic recipe, butter, eggs, and milk were readily available on the farm.

Uncle Frank's Coconut Custard Pie

Add 2½ cups coconut with butter and vanilla extract.

Johnnie Boy's Lemon Custard Pie

Substitute 3 teaspoons lemon extract for
2 teaspoons vanilla extract.

JVR '02

Judith Ralph

Parrilelee's Little Dark Cakes

½ cup brown sugar
½ cup molasses
¾ cup buttermilk
½ teaspoon salt
½ teaspoon cinnamon
½ teaspoon cloves
½ teaspoon ginger
½ teaspoon allspice
1 teaspoon baking soda
2 teaspoons baking powder
2 cups all-purpose flour
2 tablespoons shortening, melted

Add sugar and molasses to the buttermilk. Mix and sift dry ingredients and add to sugar mixture. Last, stir in melted shortening. Bake in buttered batty pans in 350 degree oven for about 25 minutes. When cool, cover with cake filling. Makes 12 cakes.

Cake Filling

8-ounce package cream cheese, softened
2 eggs
1 teaspoon vanilla
¼ cup granulated sugar
2 tablespoons flour
1 tablespoon cornstarch

Cream together cream cheese, eggs and vanilla. Mix together sugar, flour and cornstarch. Add flour mixture to the cream cheese mixture, blending well. Spread icing between cake layers.

Vicki Hawes

Lace Cookies

1 cup sorghum
1½ cups sugar
1 cup shortening
2 tablespoons cocoa
1 egg
1 teaspoon soda
½ cup hot water
1 teaspoon vanilla
1 teaspoon cinnamon
1 teaspoon cloves
1 teaspoon nutmeg

This is a word-of-mouth recipe from Lucy Magan. She told me that she got it from an "old-timer."

Cream together all ingredients. Pour by spoonfuls onto greased cookie sheet, leaving several inches between each cookie. This batter will spread all over the place. Bake at 325 degrees. To thicken batter, add cocoa or cut amount of shortening. Makes 4 dozen cookies.

Vicki Hawes

"Mom and Dad buried fruit and vegetables in the ground for the winter. Dad dug a hole and lined the bottom with hay, then threw in the turnips, potatoes, cabbages, and apples. For insulation against the cold, he added another layer of hay before filling the hole with dirt. On Christmas Day, Dad would dig a little hole and pull out some of the apples. I'll never forget how cold and crisp those Christmas apples were, especially the big red King Davids."

Norman Matthews

Mom's Schoolhouse Molasses Cookies

2 eggs
1 cup sugar
1 cup molasses
1 cup lard
1 teaspoon soda mixed in 2 teaspoon vinegar
2 to 3 cups all-purpose flour

Mix all ingredients together with enough flour to make a stiff dough. Roll out and cut into cookies. Bake at 350 degrees for 8 to 10 minutes. Makes about 3 dozen cookies.

Kathryn Bailey

"We wrapped walnuts in pretty colored foil, tied them off with yarn and hung them on the Christmas tree at Grandmother Leach's house."

Emogene Miller Moseley

Old Recipe Molasses Bars

1 cup shortening
⅔ cup brown sugar
1 cup sorghum molasses
3¼ cups all-purpose flour
2 teaspoons soda
½ teaspoon salt
1 teaspoon cinnamon
1 teaspoon ginger
¼ teaspoon ground cloves
¼ teaspoon nutmeg
1 cup buttermilk

Cream together shortening, brown sugar and molasses. Sift together the dry ingredients. Add sifted ingredients to creamed mixture, alternating with the buttermilk, beginning and ending with flour. Pour into two 15-inch jellyroll pans. Bake at 375 degrees for 15 to 20 minutes. Frost with a vanilla icing. Cut into squares. Makes 7 to 8 dozen bars.

Willa M. Spradling

"A left-over baked potato can be rebaked if you dip it in water and bake in a 350-degree oven for about 20 minutes."

Joyce Leach

'Lasses Cookies

1 cup firmly-packed brown sugar
1 egg, beaten
1 cup pure sorghum
1 teaspoon cinnamon
1 teaspoon ginger
¾ cup melted lard
¼ cup boiling water
Self-rising flour
Sorghum foam, optional

Andrew Ralph

In a large bowl mix together brown sugar, egg, and sorghum. Stir in seasonings, lard, and water, mixing well. Add enough flour to form soft dough. Spoon dough onto very lightly-greased cookie sheet. Drizzle with sorghum foam. Bake at 300 degrees for 7 to 10 minutes. These cookies were a sell-out at the 2001 Hancock County Sorghum Festival. Makes 3 dozen cookies.

For three generations our family has been making sorghum molasses. Papaw Jimmy Ralph used to save 100 gallons of molasses each year. If it weren't for the milk cow, cornbread, and sorghum molasses, the family would have starved to death some winters.

When we were kids, Daddy moved his equipment from place to place, making sorghum for other folks for a share of the molasses. Us kids dipped cane into the foam and licked it like suckers.

Today, Daddy and his brothers, Roy and Gene, continue to make sorghum molasses much the same way their ancestors did, cooking the syrup in a pan heated with wood.

Judith and Dennis Ralph

November

A season of thankfulness

*"For what thanks can we render to God again
for you, for all joy wherewith we joy
for your sakes before God."*
                    1 Thessalonians 3:0

Kathryn, Ralph and John Mitchell

Country Boy Ham and Biscuits

1 country ham, sliced thin

Hot biscuits

Remove rind and bone from ham slices. Cut remaining meat into biscuit-size pieces. Layer in a large iron skillet. Add enough water to simmer ham slices until tender. Turn as needed. When ham is done, let water cook down, then turn ham slices to slightly brown both sides. Serve on hot biscuits.

On the farm, Mamaw boiled, then baked, whole country hams for Christmas dinner. The Moseleys were quite proud of their smoked meats. I know this from the smile on Papaw's face as he pushed open the door to the meat house, then pointed out the hickory smoked hams, shoulders and bacons hanging from the ceiling. Today, country ham and biscuits is a traditional dish in our home on Christmas Eve. They are a family favorite and are quite filling for a group of hungry men.

Judith Ralph

Country Sausage

7 pounds lean pork
3 pounds fat pork
3 tablespoons salt
2 teaspoons salt
2 teaspoons sage
1⅔ tablespoons black pepper
¾ teaspoon cayenne pepper

"When we stock our freezer with homemade sausage, our youngest son Robert, counts the packages until there are none."

Cube lean and fat pork. Dennis uses a chunk of tenderloin for better texture. Spread on tabletop and season. Mix well and let stand for 10 minutes, then grind. Mix again, then grind and taste test.

To taste test: fry a sausage patty in an iron skillet. "Good" sausage will make enough grease to fry itself. Let cool, taste, add seasoning, if needed.

Note: It takes several days for the flavor to strike through.

Judith Ralph

"We killed our own meat and we always had fresh or canned sausage, hams, bacon, beef and chicken. On Saturday afternoon, Mama would sometimes go to the grocery and bring home a roll of fresh bologna. It tasted so good. I also remember her frying up a big platter of hot dogs. They were a real treat."

Charles Moseley

Country Ham with Redeye Gravy

2 cups hot strong brewed coffee
¼ cup firmly-packed brown sugar
Two 12-ounce slices boneless country ham

Stir together coffee and sugar; let mixture cool. Cook ham in a large cast-iron skillet over medium heat 5 to 7 minutes on each side or until browned. Remove ham and keep warm, reserving drippings in skillet. Add coffee mixture to skillet, stirring to loosen particles from bottom; bring to a boil. Boil, stirring occasionally, until reduced by half, about 15 minutes. Serve immediately with ham. Makes 6 servings.

Kim Mitchell

Deer Jerky

This recipe belongs to Jerry Poteet, a friend from Big Clifty, KY.

2 teaspoons chili powder
3 tablespoons brown sugar
¼ cup Worcestershire sauce
1 bottle Alegro Marinate Sauce
1½ teaspoons Tabasco sauce
1 teaspoon garlic powder
1 teaspoon onion powder
2 teaspoons salt
1 tablespoon pepper
1 pound deer meat, sliced thin

Mix first 9 ingredients together. Add deer meat slices. Marinate meat in the sauce for at least 8 hours. Place marinated meat on food dehydrator and cook according to dehydrator directions.

Ralph Mitchell

Corn Pudding

3 tablespoons butter or margarine
3 tablespoons all-purpose flour
1 tablespoon sugar
¾ teaspoon salt
¾ cup milk
17-ounce can cream-style corn
3 eggs

Melt butter in heavy saucepan over low heat; add flour, sugar, and salt, stir until smooth. Cook 1 minute, stirring constantly. Gradually add milk; cook over medium heat, stirring constantly, until thickened and bubbly. Remove from heat, and stir in corn. Beat eggs well. Gradually stir about ¼ hot mixture into beaten eggs, add to remaining hot mixture, stirring constantly. Pour into a greased 1½-quart casserole. Bake at 350 degrees for 1 hour. Makes 6 servings.

Kim Mitchell

"I tell folks that I am of Northern Irish descent - I grew up on Northern beans and Irish potatoes."

Norman Matthews

Sunday Sweet Potatoes

5 medium sweet potatoes, unpeeled
2 cups brown sugar
2 sticks butter
½ cup half and half
2 tablespoons flour
1 teaspoon cinnamon
½ cup nuts, optional

Boil potatoes covered in water until just able to pierce with fork. (Do not overcook.) Let cool. While cooling, make syrup with next 3 ingredients. Melt slowly over low heat. Peel and slice cooled potatoes, layer in large casserole dish. Sprinkle with flour and cinnamon. Pour sauce over the potatoes. Top with nuts. Bake at 350 degrees for 30 minutes.

Judy Back

These are by far the best sweet potatoes you've ever tried. Dad always saves his for dessert. Note the ingredients and you will understand why.

"I always looked forward to company on the farm. I recall one wintry day when we were expecting Aunt Myrtle to come and spend the night. My mother was sitting by the side window churning butter in an old-fashioned crock churn. I sat watching."

Emogene Miller Moseley

Cracklin' Cornbread

2 cups cornmeal
2 teaspoons salt
1 teaspoon baking soda
½ teaspoon baking powder
1 cup buttermilk
½ cup cracklin's

Combine cornmeal, salt, soda, and baking powder. Add buttermilk, stirring until smooth. Then blend cracklin's into the mixture. If too dry, add warm water to desired consistency. Pour into a 10½-inch greased cast-iron skillet. Bake in 425 degree oven until golden brown.

Cracklin's may be made by removing the skin from cooked turkey breast, then baking in the oven until crisp.

Lorene Wright

"At hog killing time, Papa would take a hog bladder, wash it real good, then turn it wrong side out and wash it again. He cut a cane pole in two at the joints and attached a bladder to one section. We blew it up like a balloon. Times were hard. Us children played with anything we could get a hold of."

"The week of my wedding, I cleaned out my closet and found several boxes of chocolate Easter rabbits and Easter lambs on the shelf. I could never eat them, because I was afraid I would ruin them."

Judith Moseley Ralph

Velma's Old-Fashioned Oyster Dressing

½ cup chopped onion
1 cup chopped celery
½ cup margarine
8-ounce can oysters, reserving liquid
8 cups dry bread cubes
½ teaspoon poultry seasoning
½ teaspoon ground sage
⅛ teaspoon salt
¼ teaspoon black pepper
1½ cups chicken or turkey broth

Sauté onions and celery in margarine until tender, but not brown. Cook oysters plus ⅓ cup of liquid in a small skillet for 8 to 10 minutes. Place bread cubes in a large bowl. Add seasonings. Stir. Add onions, celery and oysters. Drizzle 1¼ cups broth over mixture until moist. Toss lightly. Pour dressing in lightly-greased baking dish. Drizzle with remaining broth. Bake at 375 degrees for 20 to 30 minutes.

I'm not sure if it's the delicate blend of spices, the extra broth, or if it's the special memories of Mamaw that give this traditional dressing a rich, savory flavor unmatched by today's contemporary versions.

Dried Bread Cubes

Let 8 cups white bread cubes stand at room temperature for 8 to 12 hours. Or spread 8 cups white bread cubes into a single layer on a baking pan. Bake in a 300 degree oven 10 to 15 minutes until dry. Stir twice.

Judith Ralph

Sugar Glazed Cranberry Sauce

1 pound fresh whole cranberries
2 cups sugar
1½ cups water

Wash cranberries then place in large saucepan. Add sugar and water. Heat to boiling, stirring until sugar dissolves. Boil rapidly until berries pop open, approximately 5 to 10 minutes.

Emogene Moseley

Thanksgiving Ambrosia

Not just for Thanksgiving.

1 bunch bananas, peeled and sliced
20-ounce can pineapple chunks
6 oranges, peeled and sectioned or 11-ounce can mandarin oranges, drained
1 jar maraschino cherry halves
2 apples, cored and chopped
1 cup chopped pecans
1 cup flaked coconut
1 cup miniature marshmallows
½ cup honey, optional

Mix ingredients in the order listed; sweeten with honey; chill; serve.

Kim Mitchell

Granny Jean Fannin's Pecan Pie

This was given to me from Granny Jean Fannin. She was the world's best cook ever.

1 cup pecans
1 cup dark corn syrup
2 tablespoons butter
2 eggs
1 cup granulated sugar
1 teaspoon vanilla
1 unbaked pie shell

Mix together first 6 ingredient; pour into unbaked pie shell. Bake at 350 degrees for 45 minutes.

Evelyn Motley

Make your own houseplant fertilizer

1 tablespoon saltpeter
1 tablespoon Epsom salts
1 tablespoon baking powder
1 tablespoon ammonia
1 gallon water

Combine and use to water houseplants.

Willa M. Spradling

Pumpkin 'n Custard Pie

1½ cups sugar
½ teaspoon salt
4 tablespoons cornstarch
2 heaping tablespoons flour
3 teaspoons cinnamon
¼ teaspoon ginger
½ teaspoon nutmeg
¼ teaspoon ground cloves
2 tablespoons brown sugar
4 egg yolks
3 cups milk
1 large can pumpkin, about 1½ cups
1½ sticks margarine
1 teaspoon vanilla extract
2 baked pie shells

Mix the dry ingredients in a large kettle. Add the egg yolks, milk, and pumpkin to the dry ingredients in the kettle. Cook over medium heat until mixture comes to a full boil. Boil for 1 minute until mixture thickens. Remove from heat and add margarine and vanilla extract. Pour into 2 baked pie shells. Top pies with meringue.

"This is the recipe that Charles' mother always used to make her pumpkin pies for Thanksgiving. I have never seen anyone else that cooked the pie mixture on top of the stove or put meringue on top of the pies. Charles and his brothers always thought this was the only way to make a good pumpkin pie. This is the only way I have made a pumpkin pie since I got this recipe after we married. I always think about those good Thanksgiving meals at the Moseley farm, when I make my pumpkin pies for Thanksgiving."

"To reheat roast, wrap in aluminum foil and start in a COLD oven at low temperature. This keeps roast from tasting warmed over."

Joyce Leach

Meringue for 2 pies

3 egg whites
½ teaspoon cream of tartar
12 tablespoons sugar
1 teaspoon vanilla extract

Beat egg whites and cream of tartar until frothy. Gradually beat in sugar, 1 tablespoon at a time. Add vanilla. Continue beating until stiff and glossy. Spread over pies, sealing edges of crust. Bake at 400 degrees for 8 to 10 minutes.

Emogene Moseley

Sweetened Condensed Milk

⅓ cup boiling water
⅔ cup sugar
1 tablespoon butter
1 cup powdered milk

Mix together boiling water, sugar and butter. Add powdered milk and beat with mixer until smooth and dissolved. Use immediately or refrigerate unused portions.

Julie Ralph Alford

December

A season of tradition

*"…but whosoever shall do and teach them,
the same shall be called great
in the kingdom of heaven."*
Matthew 5:19

Anthony, Ralph, Daniel, Kim, Michael Mitchell

"It's No Bother"

Fifty years or more ago,
My mother tucked me in my bed;
A homemade quilt sewn with love,
A feather pillow for my head.

On cold winter nights she warmed an iron
And wrapped it in a cloth.
She put it close against my feet to keep them from the frost.

Now Mom is old and it's my turn,
To tuck her in her bed.
I wrap her feet to keep them warm,
A feather pillow beneath her head.

"I hate to be such a bother,"
she tells me now and then.
It's no bother but a joy,
To tuck my mother in.

Kathryn Bailey

Cheese Ball

1 package Cracker Barrel extra sharp cheese
Two 8-ounce packages cream cheese
1 tablespoon minced onion
2 tablespoons Worcestershire sauce
1 teaspoon lemon juice

Shred the Cracker Barrel cheese. Combine all ingredients and mix well.

Phyllis Blanton

Sausage Balls

2 pounds sausage
1½ cups biscuit mix
4 cups shredded cheddar cheese
Salt and pepper

Preheat oven to 375 degrees. Mix all ingredients. Form into 1-inch balls. Bake 15 minutes on ungreased cookie sheet. Makes 48 sausage balls.

Kim Mitchell

Ruby's Fruit Salad

1 can sweetened condensed milk
1 teaspoon lemon juice
16-ounce container whipped topping
15-ounce can crushed pineapples, drained
16-ounce can fruit cocktail, drained
1 cup pecans

Mix all together. Chill. Makes a good salad.

Ruby Vanover Ralph

Minnie Bell's Cranberry Salad

2 cups sugar
1 cup water
2½ tablespoons Knox gelatin, soaked in ½ cup cold water
4 cups raw cranberries, ground
1 orange with rind, ground
1 cup chopped celery
1 cup chopped nuts

Cook sugar and water to make thin syrup. Add soaked gelatin. Stir until dissolved. Cool. Add remaining ingredients. Pour into lightly-greased mold. Chill.

The late Minnie Bell Basham Leach

Mom's Jam Cake

1 cup shortening
2 cups brown sugar
4 eggs
1 cup blackberry jam
3½ cups flour
½ teaspoon salt
2 teaspoons baking soda
Spices to taste
1 cup raisins
1 cup chopped nuts
1 cup mincemeat
1 cup buttermilk
1 teaspoon rum flavoring
1 teaspoon brandy flavoring

Cream shortening and sugar together. Add eggs one at a time, beating after each egg. Add jam to this mixture. Sift flour, salt, soda, and spices together. Mix raisins, nuts, and mincemeat into flour mixture. Alternate flour mixture and milk to egg mixture. Stir in flavorings. Bake in a well-greased angel food cake pan for at least 2 hours at 300 degrees. Frost with a thin layer of caramel icing.

Bess Phelps 1895-1963

Caramel Icing

1 small carton cream
1 pound brown sugar
3 tablespoons butter
1 teaspoon vanilla

Mix cream and sugar well. Bring to a boil and boil for 3 minutes until a soft ball forms in cold water. Remove from heat; add butter and vanilla. Beat until cool and of spreading consistency with wooden spoon. Spread over cake.

Grandmother Hemmingway's Jam Cake

1½ cups sugar
1 cup buttermilk
2 cups jam
½ cup raisins
1 or 2 cups nuts
1 teaspoon vanilla
1 teaspoon cinnamon
2 eggs
Add flour as needed

Icing

1 cup sugar
1 cup coconut
1 stick of butter
1 cup cream
3 egg yolks

Ruby Vanover Ralph

100 year old recipe from my grandmother Hemmingway.

Ruby Vanover Ralph

"*Mama always made the best jam cake for Christmas dinner. Everybody loved it.*"

Connie Ralph Boling

Hummingbird Cake

3 cups all-purpose flour
2 cups granulated sugar
1 teaspoon salt
1 teaspoon baking soda
1 teaspoon ground cinnamon
3 eggs, well beaten
1½ cups vegetable oil
1½ teaspoons pure vanilla extract
8-ounce can crushed pineapple, undrained
¾ cup pecans
¼ cup black walnuts
2 cups chopped bananas

Combine all dry ingredients in a large mixing bowl. Add eggs and oil stirring until dry ingredients are moistened. Do not actually beat with a mixer. Stir in vanilla, pineapple and nuts. Finally, add the bananas. Spoon the batter into 3 well-greased and floured 9-inch round cake pans. Bake in pre-heated oven at 350 degrees for 25 to 30 minutes or until cake tests done. Cool in pan 10 minutes; turn onto cooling rack. Cool completely before icing with Cream Cheese Frosting.

Cream Cheese Frosting

Two 8-ounce packages cream cheese, softened
1 cup butter (not margarine), at room temperature
Two 16-ounce packages powdered sugar
2 teaspoons pure vanilla extract
1 cup chopped pecans

Combine cream cheese and butter. Cream until smooth. Add powdered sugar, beating with electric mixer until light and fluffy. Stir in vanilla. Frost tops of all 3 layers. Stack, then frost edges. Make a circle indentation on top layer. Fill circle with chopped pecans.

Kathryn Mitchell

Mamaw Allie's Butter Pie

"Mamaw Allie baked the best butter pies and big chewy cookies. Sometimes she would bake enough cookies to fill a pillowcase, then she would tie them up and hide them from us grandkids."

1 cup brown sugar
½ cup flour
1 stick butter, melted
¼ teaspoon nutmeg
¼ teaspoon cinnamon
1 unbaked pie shell

Combine first five ingredients and pour into unbaked pie shell. Mamaw always sprinkled extra cinnamom on top. Bake at 350 degrees until set.

Martha Sue Edge

"Churning butter took all day long, and us kids usually got stuck with that chore. To make time pass, we would sing, 'Churn, butter, churn. Hope that old cow dies!'"

Dennis Ralph

Emogene's Southern Pecan Pie

3 eggs, well beaten
1 cup sugar
½ cup light corn syrup
¼ cup melted margarine
1 cup pecans
9-inch unbaked pie shell

Beat eggs with mixer. Stir sugar, syrup, melted margarine, and pecans into beaten eggs. Mix well with a large spoon. Pour into unbaked pie shell. Bake 45 minutes at 375 degrees.

Emogene Moseley

"I made 2 pecan pies from this recipe for our family's Christmas dinner at my grandmother and grandfather Leach's home in the year, 1957, that I was married. I have taken 2 pecan pies to all the family holiday meals since that year."

"Potatoes will bake in a hurry if they are boiled in salted water for 10 minutes before popping into a very hot oven."

Joyce Leach

From the time she was able to reach the stove-top, Julie has enjoyed preparing special treats just for Dad.

Just For Dad Triple Decker Coconut Bars

½ cup butter
1½ cups graham cracker crumbs
7-ounce package flaked coconut
14-ounce can sweetened condensed milk
12-ounce package semi-sweet chocolate chips
½ cup creamy peanut butter

Preheat oven to 350 degrees (325 degrees for glass dish). In 9x13-inch pan, melt butter in oven. Sprinkle graham cracker crumbs evenly over butter. Top evenly with coconut, then sweetened condensed milk. Bake 25 minutes or until lightly browned. In small saucepan, over low heat, melt chips with peanut butter. Spread evenly over hot coconut layer. Cool 30 minutes. Chill thoroughly. Cut into bars. Store loosely covered at room temperature. Makes 32 servings.

Julie Ralph Alford

"Tansy, a plant originally from Egypt, grew wild on our farm. It has a yellow bloom and green feathery leaves, which are boiled for its medicinal properties. A cloth soaked in the green water, then placed on an injury, will draw out the swelling."

Hubert Oliver

Classic Fifties Chocolate Fudge

5 cups sugar
12-ounce can evaporated milk
2 sticks margarine
Pint jar marshmallow cream
Two 12-ounce packages chocolate chips
1½ cups pecans

Mix sugar, milk, and margarine in large kettle. Stir constantly until it reaches a full boil. Boil 8 minutes, stirring constantly. Remove from heat and add marshmallow cream and chocolate chips. Beat with mixer until it all melts and is blended. Add pecans and pour into a 9x13-inch pan to cool.

Emogene Moseley

"I have been making fudge from this recipe since the early 1950s. My mother got the recipe from a G.E. newsletter when she worked at the G. E. plant in Owensboro, KY. It has been a favorite for the Christmas holidays ever since."

"To clear a clogged drain pour one box of baking soda followed by vinegar into the drain."

Martha Carmon Ralph

Miss Conrad's Christmas Candy

Miss Sara Conrad was a principal and teacher at Ezel School while it was under the auspices of the United Presbyterian. To most people, this will have no meaning. Others who remember her as a tough, hard-nosed "ol' gal" will wonder about this sweet recipe. However, it is very good.

3 cups sugar
¼ teaspoon cream of tartar
¼ teaspoon salt
1 cup light cream
1 tablespoon butter

Combine all ingredients and cook to soft-ball stage. Remove from heat. Let cool until you can rest your hand on bottom of pan. Beat until it begins to thicken. Add:

1½ teaspoons vanilla
½ cup chopped nuts
¼ cup chopped dates
¼ cup candied cherries

Pour on greased plate. Let cool and cut into pieces. I leave out the dates and add ¼ cups green candied cherries.

Mary Kathryn Motley

"Buck Hobbs, he would come to our house and stay several days and flour was too high to buy. He would bring a sack of flour with him. He said he had to have biscuits to eat."

Clarence Miller

Kentucky's Best Peanut Butter Fudge

3 cups granulated sugar
1 cup brown sugar
1 tablespoon corn syrup
1 cup whipping cream
1 stick butter
1½ cups creamy peanut butter
1 cup marshmallow creme

In heavy saucepan mix first five ingredients, stirring until full boil. Turn heat down. Do not stir anymore. Cook until soft ball stage. Test by putting spoonful of candy into cold water. Test to see if a small ball forms about 240 degrees. Take from heat. Add peanut butter and marshmallow creme. Beat until thick and has lost its gloss. Pour into buttered 9x13 casserole dish. Chill and cut.

Judy Back

Judy Motley Back

" This recipe was given to me by my mother, Velma Leach Miller. I have given it to my daughter and granddaughter. We use this punch for weddings, graduations, showers, holidays, and other special events, served in a special punch bowl given to me by my daughter and son in the 1960s for Christmas."

Welcome to My Party Punch

2 packages cherry Kool-Aid
2 cups sugar
1 quart water
1 quart gingerale, chilled
46 ounces pineapple juice, chilled
½ gallon vanilla ice cream

Mix Kool-Aid, sugar and water. Add gingerale and pineapple juice. Pour mixture in punch bowl. Add ½ gallon sliced up vanilla ice cream. For green punch instead of red, use 2 packages lime Kool-Aid and 1 gallon pineapple sherbet.

Emogene Moseley

Coffee Punch

4 tablespoons instant coffee
1 cup sugar
4 cups water
1 quart milk
½ cup chocolate syrup
2 tablespoons pure vanilla
½ gallon vanilla ice cream

Heat coffee, sugar, and water until coffee and sugar are dissolved. Cool, add milk and chocolate syrup. Blend, then stir in vanilla. Refrigerate overnight. When ready to serve, add vanilla ice cream. Delicious!

Kathy Jo Motley Cole

Patience

"As a child growing up on a farm, one of the most exciting days of the year was Hog Killing Day. All of my aunts and uncles came to help with this chore that involved a tremendous amount of work and cooperation. I remember most vividly all the laughing, talking and joking that went on in the midst of all the work. No one in my family was afraid of hard work and they made even the work seem like a good time."

"For an eleven-year-old girl, all the activity was something I enjoyed and participated in eagerly. But as an adult, I look back and see one person sitting in front of the smokehouse doing what I considered at the time as the most boring job of all. Grandma Bumm was in charge of getting the sausage casings ready for the sausages that my father and grandfather ground and seasoned. She had the task of cleaning all the casings that would hold this delicious mixture of sausages. She would sit on the same stool for 2 or 3 hours washing the casings and then turning each one inside out and cleaning them again. It took me several years of growing up to realize that my grandmother was the most patient woman I have ever known. Turning those casings inside out was a tedious chore that required a skilled hand and, most of all, the endurance to sit quietly and concentrate on those slippery skins. She never complained or asked for help. She would smile at me as I came running up to see how she was doing and talk to her a few minutes. I see that smile today so many years later in my memories of her and know that she showed that patience to me many times as I grew older. She was truly a marvelous woman who showed me love and taught me many things."

Barbara Coomes

Index